Steve Gooch
and Paul Thompson

The Motor Show

Pluto  Plays

1.

The Motor Show

1. The Motor Show

[**Salesman Barker** comes on with **Dolly Bird** and rehearses his spiel for The Motor Show.]

Barker: Hi there, everyone. Welcome to The Motor Show. Once again the Big Motor Company's here in force to give away happiness and bring you freedom. For your delectation this year we're presenting the newest version of the world-famous Model Zee—or Tin Zillie as she's affectionately known. Easy to handle, she'll take all sorts of using and she's **oh**-so cheap to run. As the great and wonderful Mr Big himself says: 'A car for the great multitude.' — That's you, folks.

Dolly: Dat won't fool no-one.

Barker: Whaddayer mean?

Dolly: Dey call me a dumb broad, but even I know it's last year's model wid a fresh coat of black paint.

Barker: Will you let me finish? I gotta perfect this patter. We open this show in two hours. [He smiles and focusses on the audience again.] You've all seen them guys riding around in their big flashy limousines. Full of swank. And you say to yourself: 'I wish I could be like that.' Well you can. Cos this is the car for the little guy. [Smiles again.] Yes folks, in this car you too can feel like a million dollars as you take to the highways of the United States with the Greats. Enjoy a wonderful and better world. Join Mr Big's big happy family!

Dolly: Big deal.

Barker: Whaddayer mean?

Dolly: Even his blood relatives he hates, if dey get in his way.

Barker: Will you shut up? He could be here any minute.

[**Dolly** shrugs. He turns to the audience and smiles.]

Barker: So without further ado, I present the new 1914 Model Zee! [Nothing.] Pull the cord. [**Dolly** looks at him.] Pull the cord, dum-dum.

Dolly: What for? It ain't dere.

Barker: What ain't?

Dolly: The Model Zee.

Barker: Whaddayer mean it ain't there?

Dolly: I looked.

[**Barker** looks.]

Barker: Someone took it. Who the f- [He clamps his hand over his mouth.] Do I have to nail everything down?

George: [Off] Ahem.

Barker: Did you hear something?

George: [Off] Ahem.

1

Dolly: It's George the Foreman. I think he has something to tell y⟨

Barker: George! D'you know where the car is?

George: [Still off, mutters incomprehensibly.]

Barker: Come here, George. I can't hear you from there.

[**George the Foreman** shuffles on, shy of audience.]

Barker: Now what's happened, George? [**George** whispers shyly ⟨ his ear.] My God! [Whisper.] Gone back to the facto⟨ [Whisper.] A fault? [Whisper.] Left-hand drive. With rig⟨ hand foot-pedals?

Dolly: [Sour, to audience.] Mr Big's latest gimmick.

Barker: He'll murder us!

George: [Weeping like Stan Laurel] He'll take our jobs away!

Dolly: He's got a knack for doing that, buster.

George: But we're not to blame!

Barker: It makes no difference. He's gonna be mad and we⟨ gonna be nearest.

Mr Big: [Off] Barker!

George: [Quaking] It's him!

[Musical cue. They stare towards where the voice ca⟨ from. MR BIG, a diminutive figure, enters from the ot⟨ side. He coughs politely to draw their attention. They s⟨ round.]

Barker: Oh Mr Big, I'm so sorry, so sorry, you don't know h⟨ desolated I am.

George: And me, Mr Big. And me. Please.

Mr Big: [Soft] Why, what's the problem, boys?

Barker: A slight hitch.

Mr Big: [Soft] Oh really?

Barker: A little adjustment.

George: A fault.

Mr Big: [Roars] WHAT ? ? ! !

George: Not our fault.

Barker: A left-hand drive with right-hand foot pedals.

Mr Big: All this left and right business, it's suspicious. Poli⟨ shouldn't interfere with business. It must be sabotage.

George: No, the workers.

Mr Big: Like I say: sabotage. And I've put everything into this⟨ too. I've taken the steel from God's great earth, rubber ⟨ wood from His trees, glass from His great beaches...

Dolly: String from His garters and chewing-gum from Wrigleys⟨

Mr Big: [Soft] I beg your pardon?

Dolly: You hoid, schmuck.

2

Mr Big: [Soft] You're fired.

[**Dolly** shrugs and goes.]

Mr Big: Bad language I can't stand, Barker.

Barker: Yes, sir. No, sir.

Mr Big: Why do they do this to me? I've done everything for the workers. I've given them work. A car just for them, the great multitude. Large enough for the family, but small enough for the individual to run. So a man can enjoy the blessings of God's great open spaces. I just want to make the world a better place to live in. Don't people want to be happy no more?

George: They wanna be but they're not. [Corrects himself] Completely, that is.

Mr Big: But it's your job to keep them happy. You're the foreman.

George: That's what I tell them.

Mr Big: They're part of a miracle! Everyone who makes my car can also afford to buy it.

George: I can't.

Mr Big: A small problem, George. Learn thrift, like I did. There's always a solution. These are modern times, a scientific age. All my life I've met problems — unaccountable problems — but I've overcome them. We had a problem with the men on my Pappy's farm. So I changed them for machines. When I built my first car I couldn't get it through my landlord's barn-door. So I knocked the wall down. People called me pig-headed when I went into business, disagreed with my ideas. Competition. So I bought 'em up. It's a free world. Room for everyone. And this, my dream, the car to end all cars for 500 dollars when 10 years ago they cost 1500 — they thought I was insane. Ha!

Barker: [Unconvinced] Ha.

Mr Big: I don't understand it. Why aren't they happy?

George: It's your latest idea, sir, the production line. It's . . . it's . . . hard work.

Mr Big: I was never afraid of hard work! No man should be afraid, of hard work.

George: Last year over 50,000 men left the factory, sir.

Mr Big: But why? The idea is to make their work easy.

2. The Production Line

[Hooter. **Workers** come on and start their morning shift on the assembly line.]

Mr Big: The greatest labour-saving device ever invented. The flywheel

3

magneto assembly line. The last word in efficiency and grace
Poetry in motion.

Barker: No more heavy weights to lift and lug. No stooping. It comes to you. Fluent, smooth action, regular, easy.

George: It isn't quite like that, sir.

Mr Big: We make more cars so the worker earns more money.

George: That doesn't compensate for a nervous breakdown, sir. [He takes a pill.]

Mr Big: But there's no **mind**-work involved!

George: Right, sir, they go nuts.

Mr Big: They can think about the Model Zee they'll have earned after only 200 days in the factory!

George: They got to eat too, sir, feed their families, pay the rent.

Mr Big: [Suddenly sharp] SHOIKERS ! !

George: No sir!

Mr Big: You contradicting me, George? [He starts shadow-boxing.]

George: N-n-n-no, sir.

Mr Big: [Stops] Good.

[A **Worker** suddenly downs tools and goes.]

Worker 1: Eah, shit.

Worker 2: Wait for me.

[The **Workers** walk out.]

George: Sorry, sir.

Mr Big: Bad language, good riddance.

Barker: It **is** a problem, sir, 50,000 men lost last year. But like all your problems we'll overcome them.

Mr Big: I wanna be alone.

Barker: Yes, sir. Of course. [He and **George** go.]
[Light change]

3. Mr Big Calls on His Pappy

Mr Big: Pappy! Are you there, Pappy?

Pappy: [Appearing.] Hello, son.

Mr Big: Pappy, you know it's always you I come to in times of difficulty.

Pappy: Wanna borrow some money again, son?

Mr Big: No Pappy, it's advice I need, advice. My men don't seem to want to work for me, Pa. I thought maybe you could tell me why.

Pappy: Can I speak freely, son? I mean, I don't wanna be hurtful to yer.

Mr Big: Go right ahead, Pappy, shoot. I can take it.

Pappy: Well it's like this, son. Yer're gittin' yer agriculture wrong.

Mr Big: But I'm in motor cars, Pa, not farming.

4

Pappy: Yer're still makin' things for folk though, right?

Mr Big: Sure.

Pappy: Well, the main thing to remember is, we're all on this world together, son. In the eyes of Nature we're all equal.

Mr Big: That sounds like Bolshevism, Pa.

Pappy: Don't know what that is, son, but from where I'm looking, you men all look pretty much the same to me.

Mr Big: Go on, Pa.

Pappy: Look at it this way, son. Man's a part of Nature. He feeds the soil and the soil feeds him. But the seed you been sowin's gonna bring you a bad harvest one day, it'll be the end of your line. You're tryin' to take more out than yer're puttin' in.

Mr Big: But that's business, Pa, progress.

Pappy: Sure, son. Except if you store too much grain in your own barn you ain't gonna be popular.

Mr Big: But I don't wanna be liked, Pa. I wanna be useful.

Pappy: Trouble with that is, you ain't the only pebble on the beach. Other farmers are gonna think up their own ideas, start storin' themselves.

Mr Big: Nothing wrong with that, Pa. Competition's healthy.

Pappy: 'Cept all you farmers gonna be competin' against each other, and then you all gotta store more and you'll all be tryin' to git more out than you put in.

Mr Big: But mine is the best method, Pa.

Pappy: Except between you you're makin' the soil so poor you're headin' for the Bad Harvest, the End of the Line.

Mr Big: That's rubbish, Pa. Sentimental, old-fashioned rubbish. There is no end to my line.

Pappy: I'm just trying to help you, son.

Mr Big: If you've got an idea, you can do anything.

Pappy: Not on your own, son, you need other men.

Mr Big: With money you can do anything. Even defy Nature.

Pappy: Time for my nap now, son. I wish you luck, but I'm warnin' yer. Take it easy or it'll come back on yer.

Mr Big: Goodbye, Pa.

Pappy: Goodbye, son. [He goes.]

Mr Big: Foolish old man. — Barker!

Barker: [Appearing immediately] Sir.

Mr Big: I've got a factory, Barker, I've got money. I've got a great car and great ideas. How do I get these men to make it work?

Barker: Tell them they got to.

Mr Big: I tried that already. It don't work.

Barker: Tell 'em a little harder. [He takes out a violin-case.]

Mr Big: What's that?

5

Barker: I been taking fiddle lessons.

[Pause.]

Mr Big: I'm not a hard man, Barker. This car is pure philanthropy. want to share it with my workers. There must be a phila thropic way.

Barker: Pay 'em more.

Mr Big: PAY 'EM MORE?! They're gettin' two dollars thirty a da as it is.

Barker: Pay 'em five dollars. They'll stay then.

Why compel when you can bribe?
You don't have to put the boot in.
To turn the screws on harder
You just put a little loot in.

Mr Big: But that's givin' it away!

Barker: Not if you're gettin' better work back out of it. Men stayin longer, getting more skilled. If you pay five dollars you have the cream. You'll not only have the best car but th best workers too.

Mr Big: It's like Pappy said: the natural thing to do.

Barker: And think of the publicity. For doubling your wages you treble production and quadruple your profits.

Mr Big: Never spit into the wind
By my Pappy I was told.

Barker: Cast your bread upon the waters
It'll come back hundredfold.

Mr Big: I like it, Barker. That was a good idea of mine you just ha The Five Dollar Day!

The Five Dollar Day Song

Barker: [Sings:]

Brighten up the worker's face
And unite the human race
The Five Dollar Day makes your problems go away.
Give your workers their share
It'll pay you to care
The Five Dollar Day makes your problems go away.

Mr Big: Just a minute. I see what they get out of it, but what do get out of it?

Barker: Industrial peace!

Mr Big: I like it.

Barker: No more absentees
Only happy employees

6

And production will rise all the time.
Some rationalisation
Some job evaluation
And a tiny bit of speed-up on the line.

Mr Big: And a tiny bit of speed-up on the line.

[They are joined by the company.]

All: The five dollar bill
The five dollar thrill
The Five Dollar Day makes your problems go away.

Mr Big is The Man
Mr Big made The Plan
The Five Dollar Day makes your problems go away.

[Repeat last verse. Parade, American-style.]

4. The Ideal Big Worker

[**Joe, Al** and **Myrtle** come on, in festive mood.]

Joe: Yahoo! [He pops a champagne cork.}

Al: Five dollars a day, Joe. Gee, that really is something.

Joe: Sure. Startin' Monday. We're celebratin' in advance. [He pours **Al** a drink.] Pull the table up, Myrtle, we'll play some cards.

Myrtle: Sure, Joe.

Al: I really do envy you, Joe. I wish I worked for Mr Big. We're still gettin' a dollar ninety at General.

Joe: You'll get lucky soon, Al, don't worry. The employers are finally wising up. They've realised we ain't machines. We got feelings too. You General guys ought to ask for parity.

[They sit down.]

Joe: Here, have a cigar.

Al: Real Havana?

Joe: Nothing but the best from now on, Al. [He deals cards.] Take two.

Al: You sure landed on your feet this time, Joe.

Joe: Yup. I'm gettin' a new watch come pay-day and Myrtle's gettin' a fur coat the week after.

Myrtle: It's what I always wanted, Al.

Joe: That and marriage.

Myrtle: We can do that too now, Joe. We'll be able to buy a house

7

so we can bring up kids.

Joe: But first I'm gonna buy my own Model Zee. How about that? Made wid my own hands!

Al: It's the American Dream come true, Joe. Everyone can work his way to the top.

Joe: The sky's the limit, and no less than we deserve.

Al: Sure. You wouldn't mind gettin' up before dawn on a cold winter's morning, stooping and lifting all day, gettin' your fingernails full of grease, your lungs full of paint fumes and riskin' hospital every minute if you were paid well for it. [He sighs.] I'm out.

Myrtle: Me too.

Joe: Let Myrtle fill your glass, Al.

Al: I've still got some.

Joe: Finish it up! There's a crateful outside. [He deals.]

[**Al** finishes his glass. **Myrtle** fills it up.]

Myrtle: No more scrimping and saving, Al. We'll have plenty of everything.

Joe: Freedom, Al, dignity. I can hold my head up high. My life's my own. Goddamit!

[**Barker** comes out from under the table.]

Joe: What the —?

Myrtle: Mr Barker!

Barker: Ok, I'll have that. [He takes the cigar from **Joe's** mouth.] Nasty habit. And that. [He takes the bottle and pours it out on the floor.] Rots the brain. Now go wash your mouth out.

Joe: Whaddayer mean? What's the idea?

Barker: Clean in body, clean in mind. Mr Big don't like workers who smoke and drink, and he can't stand swearing. Goddam is swearing.

Myrtle: You can't just come into people's homes, spoiling their fun.

Barker: It's for your own good. It's you we're thinking of. D'you want the five dollars or don't you?

[No answer. He tears up the playing cards.]

No gambling neither. It's a vice. Now. You two married?

Joe: Well, er . . . it was kinda difficult, see. We never had no money.

Barker: Living in sin will not be tolerated. Put it right. Now the attitude test. Question One: Do you believe in a fair day's work for a fair day's pay?

Joe: Fair to who?

Barker: Wrong answer. Two: Do you believe every boy can become

8

President of the United States?

Joe: What, all at the same time? — Say, what's this all about?

Barker: No one gets nothin' for nothin'. For his money Mr Big wants Ideal Workers. Question Three: Are machines more efficient than men?

Joe: Well I don't know, I . . .

Barker: Which is the odd man out? Jesus Christ, God, Mr Big or **Chrysler**?

Joe: Er . . .

Barker: If a man makes four cars 13 hours a day, how many can he make 26 hours a day?

Joe: Er . . .

Barker: If an assembly line runnin' at two miles an hour makes 20 cars an hour and the speed of light is 1860 miles a second, how many cars an hour can you make before they disappear up their own exhaust pipes?

Joe: 559,800,000.

Barker: [Surprised] Very good. Religion?

Joe: Presbyterian.

Barker: Name?

Joe: Carruthers.

Barker: That Jewish?

Joe: No.

Barker: OK, good. I wanna see you on parade Monday morning at 7 am on the dot, smiling all over, buttons shining, shoes I can see my face in. From now on we got our eye on you. [He goes.]

Al: Chiche!

Joe: I mighta known there'd be a catch.

Myrtle: And you stood there and took it! What a schmuck!

Barker: [Popping his head back] I heard that, lady.

[He makes a note, then goes.]

Myrtle: To get your five dollars you gotta be a good boy.

Joe: Eah, he's just doin' his job.

Al: I hope you know what you're doin', Joe

Union Man: [Off] Hello! Anyone in?

Myrtle: What is this, Central Station already? — The door's open!

Union Man: Hi. You just had a visit from Mr Barker?

Joe: That's right.

Union Man: I thought so, from the green round your gills. Everywhere he goes, I follow. I'm from the Union. We're organising working men everywhere — or trying to. You don't have to take all this crap from Barker.

Al: [Aghast] You swore!

Union Man: Free country, ain't it? That's the point, brothers, we're supposed to be free, but we ain't strong. They can come into

	our homes, pick us off one by one and tell us how to run our lives. If we band together though, we're as strong as they are.
Al:	That I gotta see.
Union Man:	You gettin' five dollars too?
Al:	Nope.
Union Man:	Join wid your brother and you'll get it.
Al:	I am. I'm thinking of trying Big's on Monday.
Union Man:	Don't join Big's, join the Union. If you were both in the Union, you could both be free and both be earning five dollars.
Al:	Try tellin' that to General.
Union Man:	If they disagree, we strike.
Al:	And then where's your five dollars?
Union Man:	They need us more than we need them.
Al:	Speak for yourself, brother. I got a dissolute youth I wanna lead.
Union Man:	And I got a wife and three kids. Think about it. [He goes.]
Joe:	What do you think, Al?
Al:	Eah, they're crazy. I'm comin' to Big's Monday morning. See if I hit lucky.

5. The Unions' Story

Union Man:	On Monday Joe went to work as usual. He kissed goodbye to Myrtle and made his way to the plant. Al also set out for Mr Big's factory. He stood at the gate, waiting to be hired — along with ten thousand other men. It was the middle of winter. Snow coming down and Mr Big had all the hands he needed. Soon Mr Big got anxious about the size of the crowd. He decided to disperse them. Fire hoses were turned on the men.

Such was Mr Big's concern for the common man.

Meanwhile, inside the plant, things were no better for Joe either.

[**Joe** comes on and works the production line.]

The same work force was producing 17 per cent more engines than before and 70 per cent more radiators. Speed-up had arrived at Mr Big's motor plant.

[We see **Joe** sped up.]

All through the twenties there was increased competition in the automobile industry, and the line was always sped up in the frantic search for the cheaper and cheaper automobile.

[We see **Joe** sped up again.]

1927. Mr Big ran the plant flat out till May when the last Model Zee came off the line. Out of the blue the line was stopped, the plant shut down and 60,000 workers laid off.

[**Joe** suddenly stops working, looks up and is ordered off.]

Out on the streets for six months, they added a million dollars to the City's social relief bill. Some people said Mr Big was finished, squeezed out by competition. Others thought he'd gone crazy. But most didn't know what to think.

[**Mr Big** and **Barker** are discovered in conversation.]

Barker: What next, Mr Big? Where do we go from here?
Mr Big: I never thought this would happen. One car to end all cars. That was the dream. But they stopped buying them.
Barker: How we gonna get rid of 'em, Mr Big?
Mr Big: People still have faith in me. We load 'em off on my trusted dealers and distributors. Realise our assets and start production on a new model in our factory at Crimson Creek.
Barker: New machines! A new automobile!
Mr Big: Even though it hurts.
Barker: A new beginning!

[They go.]

Union Man: 1928. Mr Big opened the Crimson Creek plant producing the new model. Better machines, fewer men and more efficiency on the line. With Barry Hennett's Service Department to keep discipline, he introduced a new concept in labour relations: no talking on the line!

[**Joe** and **Al** come on and work the line.]

Union Man: Suddenly he found himself employing ventriloquists.
Joe: Hey, Al, your flies are undone.
Al: I know. The buttons got ripped off by a door-handle.
Joe: So they even do circumcision here too!
Barker: No talking! It's subversive.
Union Man: The Five Dollar Day was a long way away. The men began to realise the need for a union. As men do when times are bad. But there's nothing so bad it can't get worse. 1929 the Wall Street crash. Unemployment grew, wage cuts the order of the day. Mr Big realised he had to keep the men outside the gates.
1932, three thousand unemployed workers marched in protest

11

to Crimson Creek. They were met by the machine guns
the city police and the Service Department of Barry Henne
Four hunger marchers were killed. Such was their conce
for the common man.

But the Union of Automobile Workers was not deterre
Men from the UAW distributed leaflets outside the gates
and were beaten up. So women took over the leaflets — ar
they too were beaten up. This led to a pitched battle betwee
the Union and Hennett's men on the Overpass leading in
the factory. One of the principal figures on the UAW si
was Walter Reuther:

Reuther: Seven times they raised me off the concrete and threw n
down on it. They pinned my arms and shot short jabs
my face. I was punched and dragged by my feet to tl
stairway. I grabbed the railings as they wrenched me loose.
was thrown down the first flight of iron steps. Then the
kicked me down the other flight of steps until I found myse
on the ground, where I was beaten and kicked.

Union Man: Mr Big was in business, competitive business, and he didn
want trade unions interfering with his freedom. They w:
hard times for everybody.

6. The Carmakers' Pool Table

[Sing]

**General
and Chrysler:**

The story of many a wasted youth
Often starts in pool rooms — that's the truth
But the wasted youth has only himself to blame
Because the fact is
If he don't practise
Then the wasted youth will never improve his game.

The wasted youth has only himself to blame
The wasted youth has only himself to blame
Because the fact is
If he don't practise
Then the wasted youth will never improve his game.
Because the fact is
If he don't practise
How the hell does he think he'll ever improve his game?

[**General** and **Chrysler,** with cues, are playing pool. **General**
is enjoying a long lucky break.]

12

Chrysler: Dese is hard times huh, General.

General: De boys is gettin' really restless, Chrysler. [He plays a shot.]

Chrysler: Always asking for more. Never satisfied with their weekly share out, dey laugh in your face.

General: [Playing a shot] Tings is gettin' serious, Chrysler.

Chrysler: I told 'em: no use dem gettin' ideas of sharin' de action. Dere's hardly room for you an' me now, let alone anyone else musclin' in.

General: Like Big, you mean?

Chrysler: Him? He's finished.

General: Sucked dry. Like dis town. [He plays a shot.]

Chrysler: What a joik.

General: If he don't like de heat, he should stay outa de kitchen. [He plays a shot.]

Chrysler: Go some place else.

General: Don't tell him dat, he might get ideas.

Chrysler: If you're gonna survive in dis business, you gotta broaden your horizons.

General: Sure. Like I took my holidays in Europe dis year. [He lines up a shot.]

Chrysler: So did I.

[General miscues.]

General: [Recovering.] No point in staying' in one place all de time. One country.

Chrysler: Or one continent for dat matter. [He plays a shot.]

General: Like your style, Chrysler.

Chrysler: If you play wid a maestro, General, you loin a few tricks. [Devastating shot.]

General: Hey! Leave some for me, will ya? We're playin' de same game here, Chrysler. We don't need to tread on each other's toes.

Chrysler: Sure. If we're playin' on a bigger table, dere's room for de two of us. [He lines up a shot.]

General: Just.

[Chrysler miscues.]

Chrysler: And Big?

General: Forget de guy. He's so small now, I can hardly see him. [He plays a shot.]

Chrysler: Today Detroit, tomorrow de woild.

[Big comes in with Barker.]

Mr Big: Hi fellas!

Chrysler: Who's dis? Paul Newman?

Mr Big: Hi General. Hi Chrysler. So dis is where you guys hang out.

General: How's a country hick like you find his way to a terrible joint like dis?

Mr Big: Barker drove me.

13

Mr Big: I'm not a young man any more. It's hard for an old dog to learn new tricks. You heard what they called me: old-timer.

Barker: They were talking about a bigger table, Mr Big. They both took their holidays in Europe this year.

Mr Big: What do you mean?

Barker: They must've found new markets. They're expanding. We gotta do the same.

Mr Big: Become a gangster you mean? Me? I'm a nice guy.

Barker: We gotta do like they do, dress like they do. Talk like they do. Go where they go. To survive.

Mr Big: [Gulp]

Barker: Fight back. Use their methods. Hit 'em where it hurts.

Mr Big: I don't now nothing no more. [He begins wandering off]. What kind of a world is this? I didn't wanna harm anybody, but now they're putting me out of business. Where's the sense in that? I gotta do something. I gotta show these guys. [He goes.]

Barker: We ain't licked yet, Mr Big. [To audience] What a cruel world. [He sings:]

The Song of Expansion

The Big Fish eats the Little Fish
That's how he stays alive
If the Little Fish likes living
He better learn how to survive
He better get bigger
That's what I figure
Bigger and bigger and bigger.

The bigger you are, my friend
The longer you live in the end
That's the way life is planned
We need room to expand
We gotta get bigger
That's what I figure
Bigger and bigger and bigger

[**Mr Big** comes back on, dressed gangster-style.]

Barker: What a transformation, Mr Big! That's more like it. Now we'll show 'em. We too can expand!

Mr Big: But, er, where are we expanding to?

Barker: Some place they would never think of.

Mr Big: Somewhere quiet. Somewhere olde worlde, with lots of tradition.

Barker: And unemployment.

Mr Big: Somewhere nice.

Barker: And cheap labour.
Mr Big: Somewhere peaceful.

7. Big's Comes to Dagenham

[Bird song. **Sid** and **Reg,** two Cockneys, sitting fishing, sing

> There ain't no work in this town any more
> There ain't no money, everybody's poor
> There are no happy blokes
> And there's no-one telling jokes
> In Dagenham!
>
> But ain't it lovely to live beside the river
> Don't it give you that special kind of shiver
> I think I'll take a swim
> And I fancy staying in
> I fancy staying in until I drown
>
> We ain't depressed, we do our best
> This lovely town don't get us down
> I think I'll take a swim
> And I fancy staying in
> I fancy staying in until I drown
>
> But ain't it lovely to live beside the river
> Don't it give you that special kind of shiver.

Reg: 'Ad a bite yet, Sid?
Sid: Not a tickle, Reg, nothin'.
Reg: I sometimes wonder if there's any fish left in this bleedin' river.
Sid: Them that are's poisoned.
Reg: Least with all that detergent flowin' out the chemical factory they ought a be clean.
Sid: Don't you believe it. I spotted a fish in Barking Creek yesterday, coughin' 'is roe up.
Reg: Surprised yer could even see 'im.
Sid: Be takin' 'em out in cans soon. You'll 'ave nuts an' bolts on your stall 'stead a whelks an' mussels.
[Great clanking, coughing, spluttering, honking, back-firing sound of a car approaching. It halts with a screech of tyres
Reg: Jesus Gawd Almighty, whass that?
Sid: Motor vehicle, en it.
Reg: Looks more like a bleedin' tank.
Sid: One a them American jobs.
Reg: Blimey, whass that inside it? Coupla coat-'angers on stilts

Sid: It's yer Capone style that, en it. Chicago gangsters an' that.

Reg: What they doin' 'ere then, scarin' the fish off.

Sid: What fish?

Reg: Watch yerself, they're comin' this way.

Sid: Preten' yer asleep.

Reg: Right.

[**Barker** and **Mr Big** come on.]

Barker: Hi there!

[**Sid** and **Reg** snore lightly.]

Barker: Hello!

[The same.]

Barker: [To Big] Quaint, huh?

Mr Big: [Roars] WE'RE TALKIN' TO YER ! !

Reg: Gaw blimey, what you tryin' a do, fella? Put the telephone out a business?

Barker: Er no, we're here in Dagenham Marshes on a very important mission, gentlemen. The famous Big Motor Company of the United States, owned largely by Mr Big himself here —

Sid: Charmed.

Barker: — is planning to build a new factory for Britain right here on this site.

Reg: What, where we been fishin'?

Barker: That's right.

Reg: What we goin' a do then? Drag net the swimmin' baths?

Barker: You could work in the factory.

Sid: Oh yeh?

Barker: Pleasant, modern conditions. Clean, spacious, warm in the winter — I understand you have no central heating over here.

Reg: What sort of work is it then?

Barker: Oh — interesting work. Technological. Plenty of it.

Mr Big: Dere sure is.

Barker: And well-paid too. Do you know America has the highest wages in the world?

Mr Big: I understand dere's a lot of unemployment over here.

Reg: Oh, we get by, guv, thanks.

Barker: Well I know you're gonna just love working in our brand new factory.

Sid: 'Oo said we're goin' a be workin' in it?

Mr Big: What else you gonna do? We'll be all over de place.

Reg: No. No thanks. We don't like Americans very much.

Mr Big: [Menacing.] Whaddayer mean?

Barker: [Quickly interceding.] Oh no, this'll be a truly English factory. An English factory for England. It's only the money going into it that's American.

17

Mr Big: An' the money comin' out.

[They laugh.]

Barker: Hey, shall we show them our lord, Mr Big. We got a rea
English lord in the car, fellas. We know you're gonna lov
him. I'll get the hamper. [He goes off.]

[Awkward pause. **Sid, Reg** and **Mr Big** eye each other wit
nervous suspicion.]

Reg: [Referring to **Big's** violin-case.] On the fiddle, are yer?
Mr Big: All de time.

[Pause.]

Mr Big: [Referring to their rods.] Fishing-rods is inefficient. If yo
put a positive charge dis side o' de river, an' a negativ
charge dat side, you could blast de fish out.
Reg: [Aside to **Sid.**] Right little charmer we got 'ere, Sid.

[**Barker** returns with the hamper.]

Barker: Here we are. We keep him in here so he don't go limp i
your damp air. [He calls] Sir Merciful!

[**Merciful Merry,** a ventriloquist's dummy, pops upright.]

Merry: Oh here we are! We're here! How spiffing!
Barker: Sir Merciful, I'd like you to meet the boys — what's you
names, fellas?
Sid: Sid, son.
Reg: Reg.
Barker: That's Sid and Reg, Sir Merciful. Say hello to Sid and Reg
Merry: Hello Sid, hello Reg. Awfully nice to meet you, I'm sure.
Barker: You have such nice manners over here. We were wondering
Sir Merciful, if Sid and Reg mightn't like to work in ou
factory.
Merry: Which factory?
Barker: The one we're building here, Sir Merciful. You're helping u
with it, remember?
Merry: Of course. How silly. Do come and work here, chaps. Joll
nice place you know, simply spiffing. [To **Barker.**] That th
sort of thing?
Sid: You workin' 'ere, Sir Merciful?
Merry: Oh I dare say they'll find a use for me somewhere, what
Sort of managerial capacity, don't ye know.
Reg: I'm sure you'll be a lot of use too, Sir Merciful.
Merry: Oh well, one does one's best, doesn't one. Eh, what? Ha-ha
Barker: We're very pleased with him.

Reg: I should think so too.

Barker: Even an English lord has to realise that the old must stand aside for the new. Man must progress. This country needs investment, and we're prepared to provide it. The days of your Empire are over.

Mr Big: Now it's my Empire. You're all washed up, boys.

Barker: A new era for Britain! Transatlantic fraternity! Mr Big comes to Essex!

Sid: Looks like our fishin' days are over, brother.

Mr Big: An' mine are just beginnin'.

[**Sid** and **Reg** go off. **Barker** calls after them.]

Barker: See you seven o'clock Monday morning, boys!

[**Big** and **Barker** reprise **The Song of Expansion**:]

> The bigger you are my friend
> The longer you live in the end
> That's the way life is planned
> We need room to expand
> We better get bigger.
> That's what I figure
> Bigger and bigger and bigger.

[At the end of the song **George, The English Foreman,** comes on and stands diffidently to one side. They don't see him. Then:]

8. The First Cruel Cut

George: [Quietly] Ahem.

Mr Big: Hey Barker, we're bein' watched.

Barker: Who's de weedy-lookin' schmuck wid de frog in his throat. Merry?

Merry: Er, one of the workmen, I think. [Looks closer.] — Oh, it's George the Foreman. [Re-assuring to **Big** and **Barker**]—On our side.

Mr Big: Ask him what he wants.

Merry: Er, what's the trouble, George old fella?

George: [Mumbles incoherently.]

Merry: Er, speak up, George, there's a good chap. We all want to hear.

George: Oh. Well it's like this, gentlemen. We've got a bit of a problem.

Merry: Oh come now, I'm sure we haven't, George. Problem?

19

Ha-ha. Nothing we can't sort out, I'm sure.

George: It's the new car, sir.

Merry: New car? What's wrong with it?

Mr Big: Nuttin's wrong wid it.

George: No, right, sir, nothin's wrong with it, nothin' at all. It's lovely car, really nice. The trouble is, it ain't movin'. Bit a bottleneck. It's all this depression there's been, unemplc ment. The costs are goin' up an' people can't afford to b it.

Mr Big: Make de car cheaper. Cut de wages.

Merry: Oh, do we have to? I mean, isn't that a little hard on t chaps?

Mr Big: Cut de wages. Sixpence an hour — or I cut yours.

Merry: Well George, it looks as though we're all going to have tighten our belts, what?

George: Do what?

Merry: Er, pull in our horns.

George: Eh?

Mr Big: Cut deir wages. Sixpence an hour.

George: They won't — [He gulps.] — they won't like that, sir.

Mr Big: Who cares what dey don't like? Dey gotta loin to lump

Merry: After all, George, money isn't everything.

George: No?

Mr Big: [To **Barker**] I like dis guy.

Merry: One has to think of the country as a whole. Good o England.

Mr Big: Dat's a nice line.

George: Oh I see. Will you be takin' a cut too then, Sir Merciful?

Merry: Sorry? What was that?

George: You, sir. Sir Merciful Merry, managing director. Will y be takin' a cut?

Merry: Oh I see. You mean me myself personally.

George: Er, yes.

Merry: Ah I see.

[Pause.]

George: Eh?

Merry: [Vacant] Sorry?

George: I'll tell the men. [He goes.]

Mr Big: An' tell 'em good!

Merry: He took that quite well, I thought.

Mr Big: Very pleasant little fella.

Merry: I don't think you'll find the men hard to get on with, N Big. Very reasonable people you know, the English.

Mr Big: I'm glad to hear it.

[Immediately, off, **Marching Workers** start chanting:]

> Not a penny off the pay
> Not a minute on the day
> Bollocks to Mr Big! Oi!

[Chanting, they come into the body of the hall, then sit down.]

Merry: Er, what do I do in this situation exactly? Call the police?

Mr Big: Not yet. Try an' get a representative. A representative's always a good idea.

Merry: What, a sort of class-monitor you mean. Sort of prefect — I say, what a terribly good name for a car.

[Shouts from **Workers,** including:]

Worker 1: Whass the idea, cuttin' our wages like this?

Worker 2: We wan' our tanner back.

Union Man: Daylight bloody robbery.

Merry: I say! I say! No good everyone speaking at once. Do you have a representative? Someone to speak for you.

[**The Workers** confer.]

Worker 2: Whass'e on about, speak for us? There's nothin' t' discuss. He's got my tanner an' I wan' it back.

Worker 1: If 'e wants t' talk to us, let 'im come over 'ere.

Union Man: Now look, lads. One of us 'as got a go an' meet 'em. It's no skin off 'is nose if we starve t' death.

Worker 1: Probably what 'e's waitin' for. The weaker we get, the stronger 'e gets.

Worker 2: Well then, 'oo's goin'?

Worker 1: Not me.

Worker 2: Nor me.

Worker 3: I ain't. Can't understan' a word 'e says.

Worker 1: Looks like you're elected, Jack.

Union Man: I don't wan' a do it.

Worker 2: 'Oo else is there?

[**Union Man** stands up.]

Merry: Oh splendid. [To **Barker** and **Big**] What now?

Mr Big: Ask him if he'd like to go for a little ride to discuss tings.

Merry: Er well, Representative, I'm sure we can work this little difficulty out, aren't you? Find an amicable solution. Mr Big's very kindly offered us the loan of one of his automobiles for a spin out in the country to discuss matters. Like to come?

[**Union Man** turns to **Workers.**]

Worker 1: Takin' yer for a ride, are they?

Worker 2: Watch 'im Jack. You're talkin' for all the lads, remember.

Worker 3: Don't let 'im rob us.

[**Union Man** joins **Big** and **Merry,** who take him off.]

Barker: Well friends, only a slight delay. Just a hitch. You wouldn care to go back to work now, while they're sorting thing out? Mm?

[No response.]

Barker: Fine, well, we'll just wait. I'm bound to say things have gon very well indeed for the company since we came here. We' very very pleased we came, and I guess you're pretty please too, huh?

[No response.]

Barker: Well quite. It's a difficult time just at the moment. — O here they are. Back again.

[**Merry, Union Man** and **Mr Big** come back on.]

Merry: We've had a good long talk, chaps, weighed all the pr and cons, and decided on a threepence an hour rise.

Mr Big: On de sixpence an hour cut. [He goes.]

Union Man: Victory ! !

Worker 1: Victory?

Union Man: Victory!

Worker 2: Victory?

Union Man: [Matter-of-fact] Victory. In the circumstances. [He joi **the Workers** again. They disperse, discussing the cut.]

Worker 1: Whass the game? They still done us out a threepence.

Union Man: Best I could do. They got all the cards in their 'ands. The know we can't last out for ever.

Worker 2: Not with a family an' rent.

Worker 3: Course, those bastards don't starve, do they.

Barker: Well fellas, I guess you're pretty pleased. Things not as ba as they seemed, huh? That's fine, that's splendid. Back work now, fellas, and let's hope we can get production r real high once again, so there's plenty for all!

Union Man: Sorry, lads.

Worker 2: Well, you did your best.

Union Man: At least this way we live to fight another day. But we got build the union.

Worker 1: Too bloody right.

Union Man: Get really strong. Then they can't do this to us.

[**The Workers** go off.]

22

Merry: Thought that went off rather well, didn't you?

Barker: You're doing just fine, Sir Merciful. Just fine.

[They go.]

Merry: [Sings:]

> I'm a merry little English aristocrat
> With an old school tie and a cricket bat
> A blazer of many different hues
> I am good news
>
> Good news for the USA
> I'll do whatever they might say
> I'll take good care of the motor plant
> While they're away
>
> Every day they're away
> I get thanks from the Yanks
> Cos there's profit in the banks
> And that's good news
>
> I am ecstatically happy
> Despite those left-wing chappies
> Despite the strikes, the unemployment queues
> I am good news
>
> Good news for the USA
> I'll do whatever they might say
> I'll take good care of the motor plant
> While they're away
>
> Oh yes.

9. New Deal

[**Mr Big,** alone.]

Mr Big: I don't understand it. Sure there's a depression, sure the market's declining, sure there's wage cuts and unemployment. But why do these people whine about it? Do I whine about it? No! When everyone else was pulling in their horns, I brought out yet another car, the V-800. Bigger and better than ever before. And the people who weren't depressed bought it. Can't these people stand on their own two feet? Trying to gang together in unions, striking all the time. They're cowards. They even sit down in the factory so I can't get workers in who do wanna work! Like everyone else

they're interfering with my freedom, my right to manage
I think fit!

[**Miss New Deal,** a reporter, comes on.]

New Deal: Mr Big! Oh Mr Big!

Mr Big: [Aside.] Who's dis broad?

New Deal: I'm from the Detroit City News.

Mr Big: [Aside.] Ah! A little lady from de newspapers come to inn
view me about my good woiks. [He smiles at her.] Alwa
happy to oblige the woild wid de good news dat is ▮
empire.

New Deal: Mr Big, I'm investigating a rumour that throughout Pre
dent Roosevelt's New Deal administration you've consisten
refused to adhere to the Automobile Code.

Mr Big: I never refused! The President's gotta right to run de cou
try just like I gotta right to run my own business. I do
mind what he does, long as he leaves me alone.

New Deal: But aren't you in favour of the fixed minimum wages a
legislation against cut-throat price-cutting as recommend
by the National Recovery Plan?

Mr Big: I got my own national recovery plan. It's called de ▮
Hospital. I'll show you around.

[They start walking.]

Mr Big: You have to realise, Miss, that the weekly wage in my fa
tory is still 50 per cent above the national average.

New Deal: But your wages are seasonal, Mr Big. When business is go▮
your workers earn more than average, but when it's b▮
they're out of work.

Mr Big: Dat's something you can't control. De market's de mark▮
My men already work a mere 35-hour week, with overti▮
when the market's good, and yet I still produce and beli▮
in cheap cars for de modest family budget. In dis resp▮
President Roosevelt's desire to legislate against de mar▮
is unconstitutional.

New Deal: But the President's concern, Mr Big, is for the casualties
market fluctuations.

Mr Big: You mean, human beings ain't perfect? Sure, dat is
problem. But we run dis hospital on factory lines. Ea▮
component in production should pay its way and
self-sufficient. We run dis hospital to give de maximum
service at de minimum of cost. We're not in de business
charity.

New Deal: So you regard the President's support of free collecti▮
bargaining as charity.

Mr Big: How can you bargain collectively? All dese unions — d▮

24

don't even recognise each other. Fighting amongst demselves over who's boss. Dere's only one boss — de market. And it doesn't lie.

[A **Worker With One Leg,** accompanied by **Doctors,** comes round on the Production Line.]

New Deal: So what's the market-value of a man with only one leg?

Mr Big: Waste not, want not. Even without his leg we can find a suitable function for him.

Worker: He don't allow unions, Ma'am. We got no protection. You get that down. He don't allow unions!

[**The Doctors** carry the **Worker** off, screaming.]

New Deal: Is this your idea of recovery, Mr Big?

Mr Big: A temporary malfunction. You have to tink of my other good works. The Big Foundation, founded to pour millions of dollars into scientific, educational and charitable activities. All for the public good.

New Deal: It also helps you avoid death duties and keep the business in the family.

[**Mr Big** coughs.]

New Deal: Besides putting a good face on your disgusting labour relations.

Mr Big: [Coughing.] Excuse me, I need a glass of water.

New Deal: Thank-you for your views, Mr Big. I shall make all this as widely known as possible. The nation will decide! [She goes.]

Mr Big: Now even de Press is against me.

10. Mr Big Calls on Pappy a Second Time

Mr Big: Pappy! Pappy! Are you there?

Pappy: As always, son, as always.

Mr Big: It's all goin' wrong, Pappy. They're all gangin' up against me. The unions, the government, my competitors — the whole world. Why don't they love me, Pa?

Pappy: If you'd listened to me before, son, you'd know why. You an' them other farmers I was tellin' you about keep competin', keep storin' more an' more in your barns an' all yer're doin' is ruinin' the soil.

Mr Big: Godammit, Pa, tell me something I can use. I ain't a farmer, I'm a motor-car manufacturer.

Pappy: Still makin' a bad harvest for people, son.

Mr Big: You mean, this is the end of the Line, Pa? The Bad Harvest?

25

Pappy: Not yet, son. But you should listen to the government, b⟨
They're on your side.

Mr Big: The government? They're just interferin', Pa!

Pappy: No, son. The government can see you an' all the otf
farmers goin' bust, farm-workers starvin', an' they're j⟨
tryin' to regulate it all.

Mr Big: Regulate it? What good are rules, Pa? Law never does ar
thing constructive.

Pappy: These rules are good for you, son. Make people for⟨
your mistakes. If you had any sense, son, you'd follow t
same path as the government.

Mr Big: What path's that, Pa?

Pappy: Diversify, son. Rotate your crops. Don't put all your e⟨
in one basket. That way you can keep on like you are ⟨
folks'll thank you for it too.

Mr Big: Gee, Pa, thanks. That sounds like a good idea.

Pappy: Course it makes no difference in the end. Bad Harves⟨
gonna come anyway. Just a matter of puttin' it off. Y⟨
farmers are still takin' more out than yer're puttin' in.

Mr Big: What d'you mean, Pa?

Pappy: Sorry, son, it's time for my nap again. I'll talk to /y⟨
another time.

Mr Big: But Pa! [Silence.] Pa! — What the hell's he talking abou⟨

11. The War

[Explosions, aeroplanes, sound effects of war.]
What's dat? Is dis de Bad Harvest? De end of de nev
ending Line?

[**Barker** wheels on the company's assets.]

Barker: Mr Big! Mr Big! Are you there, sir?

Mr Big: Over here.

Barker: What's happening?

Mr Big: I don't know.

Barker: I've brought the company's assets with me, sir. For sa⟨
keeping. The entire wealth of the Big Organisation.

Mr Big: Good tinking.

Barker: I'm frightened, sir.

Mr Big: Me too, Barker.

[**Two Workers** cross the stage as **Big** and **Barker** huddle
together in fright.]

Worker 1: This is it, pal. Everybody out.

Worker 2: And this time we stay out. Till we get recognition.

Mr Big: Dose are my workers! From Crimson Creek.

Barker: Leave it to me, sir — Hold on, you guys, where you goin'?

Worker 1: Home.

Worker 2: It's a walkout, Mr Barker. If Mr Big won't recognise our union, we won't recognise him.

Barker: But fellas, you can't do this to us. These are troubled times. Families should stick together in troubled times. Do you want more money? We'll give you a raise.

Worker 2: We don't wanna raise, we wanna union.

[**The Workers** go.]

Mr Big: What happened, Barker?

Barker: They refused my offer, sir.

Mr Big: What is dis? — Dere's another one.

[**Worker** crosses.]

Barker: Can I try a different method this time, sir?

Mr Big: Anything.

[**Barker** blocks **The Worker's** path.]

Barker: What's the idea, punk? Get back to work.

Worker: Every major motor company in the States has accepted unionisation except Big. What he's doing is against Section 7a of the National Recovery Act.

[**Barker** knees him in the crutch.]

Barker: Don't be disrespectful, punk. Where's your gratitood?

Worker: Get stuffed.

[**Barker** smashes him down.]

Barker: Get back to work now or you can say goodbye to your job.

Worker: You're too late, Barker. There's 50,000 men walked out of Crimson Creek. And you can't stop all of us. [He goes.]

Barker: I'm sorry, Mr Big. I did my best.

Mr Big: [Clutching his assets.] Dey's after dis, dat's what. Dey want my assets.

[**Miss New Deal** comes on.]

New Deal: Mr Big! Oh Mr Big!

Mr Big: Oh no. Not dat dumb newspaper broad again.

New Deal: I'm so glad I've caught you, Mr Big. [Sees the assets.] You weren't thinking of leaving the country, were you?

Mr Big: Coitainly not. I'm a patriot.

New Deal: Well, I guess now's the time to show your true patriotism.

Mr Big: Whaddayermean?

New Deal: Why, the war of course. The war in Europe.

Mr Big: War?

Barker: War?

Mr Big: No-one told me.

Barker: So dat's what it is.

Mr Big: [Caressing his assets.] I'm a pacifist. Always have been. T[o] me it's a matter of de strictest principle. Only governmen[t] and armaments manufacturers can profit from war.

New Deal: So you won't be accepting Rolls Royce's offer to help bui[ld] engines for English Spitfires and Hurricanes?

Mr Big: What offer? — Coitainly not. It's not our war, is it?

New Deal: The English are going to need trucks, jeeps and tanks, M[r] Big.

Mr Big: Really?

Barker: Say, we've got German factories too, Mr Big. We could buil[d] for both sides.

Mr Big: Barker, I'm ashamed of you.

New Deal: I take it then you're still against working in co-operatic[n] with the government and the labour unions.

[**A Worker** crosses.]

Mr Big: Of course. I . . .

Barker: Shall I . . . [He picks up his violin case.]

Mr Big: Not just now.

New Deal: How will you continue making automobiles without worker[s] Mr Big?

Mr Big: Whaddayermean?

New Deal: They're on strike, I believe.

Mr Big: Look, Miss Smartypants, I don't expect you to understan[d] but it's a matter of principle. I don't like unions.

New Deal: I still don't see how you can operate without labour.

Mr Big: Look, leave de brain-woik to me.

Barker: He's a genius, Ma'am.

New Deal: Does he know the Japanese have captured Malaya whe[re] his rubber comes from?

Mr Big: What?

New Deal: Does he know there's a steel shortage, an oil shortage, an[d] gas is soon to be rationed?

Mr Big: What's dat?

New Deal: The word is that all private motor-car production is soon t[o] be placed under Government restriction.

[Pause.]

Mr Big: I'm finished, Barker. I'm all washed up. [Looks up.] Yo[u] were right, Pappy. I'm in the valley of the shadow of deat[h] Without a staff or a hot-rod to comfort me.

[Pause. **Government Official** steps up.]

Official: Mr Big?

Mr Big: I was he.

28

Official: Message from the government. [He holds it out.]

Mr Big: What do they want now? [He takes it in desultory fashion, reads, and gets more and more excited as he does so.] '300 million dollar contract to develop 2000 horsepower 18 cylinder radial aircraft engine for Pratt and Whitney ... !

Barker: Yahoo!

Mr Big: Tell de President I'll be happy to oblige. — Clear de car park, Barker. We'll have a new plant dere in six months.

[**Another Official** steps up.]

Official 2: Mr Big?

Mr Big: [Snatching the message] B-24 Liberator bombers! Clear de soya bean field on my farm, Barker. We go into production in three months!

Barker: Right away, sir. [He goes.]

[**Third Government Official** comes up.]

Mr Big: [Snatching the message.] Trucks.

[And a **Fourth Government Official**.]

Mr Big: Jeeps!

[And a **Fifth**, with **Barker**.]

Mr Big: Buzz-bombs! It's like de good old days! Endless production! War — de ultimate form of built-in obsolescence! Dose weren't bangs we were hearin', Miss New Deal, dey were booms!

New Deal: But what about your principles, Mr Big? You said you were anti-war.

Mr Big: I was wrong. A man makes mistakes. In times of need I'm as patriotic as de next man.

New Deal: And the unions?

Mr Big: Now we're all one big happy family together, I don't see why de unions shouldn't be part of dat family too. I'll even collect deir dues for 'em.

New Deal: I believe collecting dues is one of the traditional ways for the men to pass on news and organise.

Mr Big: Is dat a fact? Well, in dese troubled times, Miss New Deal, we have to loin to trust one another.

New Deal: That's so true, Mr Big. Thank-you.

[**English Government Official** comes up.]

E. Official: Mr Big?

Mr Big: De same.

E. Official: I'm from the English government.

Mr Big: [Snatching his message.] Tin helmets, great!

Barker: We're all ready to go, sir.

War Song

[Sung by **Big**, **Barker**, **New Deal** and **Government Officials**.]

29

We've got no time to reason why
We know where our real interests lie
We shall save the economy
We'll become one big happy family

Do your bit, join hands together
Then together we can surely win the war
Do your bit, join hands together
I'll do my bit if you do yours .

12. The War in England

[To one side, **Harry** and **Lil** say goodbye.]

Lil: Ooh Harry, this is a lovely way to spend an evening.

Harry: Now is the hour, I'm afraid, Lil. I'm off tomorrow — ov‍
there.

Lil: Never mind, Harry. Pack up your troubles in your kit ba‍

Harry: I will, Lil. Course, you know I'll always be in love with yo‍

Lil: And me with you, Harry. I'll keep the home fires burnin‍

Harry: That's right, gel. We'll meet again.

Lil: There'll be bluebirds over the white cliffs of Dover.

Harry: We'll get lit up when the lights go up in London.

Lil: Listen to the nightingales in Berkeley Square.

Harry: And I'll be seeing you in all the old familiar places.

Lil: Long as you watch out for those Mamselles from Arme‍
tiers.

Harry: Don't worry, gel. You're my only sunshine. The girl I le‍
behind me. You just watch out for them Yankee Dood‍
Dandies.

Lil: I will, Harry. Goodbyee.

Harry: Goodbyee. [He goes.]

[**Barker** approaches **Lil**.]

Barker: Excuse me, Ma'am, I couldn't help overhearing that ver‍
tender moment. — Oh, d'you wear these? [He gives her
pair of nylons.]

Lil: [Taking them.] Blimey, these GIs. Don't waste no time, d‍
you. Let 'im get down the garden path. [She waves t‍
Harry.]

Barker: You misunderstand my motives, Ma'am.

Lil: Oh. I thought it was my lucky day.

Barker: It is. I was very moved by that little scene. I guess things‍
be pretty hard for you now.

Lil: Yes. Lot of hard things I'll have to go without now.

Barker: I expect now Harry's no longer on the job, you could do with one yourself.

Lil: Bit extra on the side you mean?

Barker: Everyone has to find new positions in a war. I guess you'll want to keep it warm for him.

Lil: Oh I say!

Barker: His position on the floor I mean.

Lil: 'Ere, exactly what are you on about?

Barker: His job on the line, Ma'am. Make sure no-one muscles in while he's away. Earn a little nest-egg, a surprise for the conquering hero.

Lil: Who, Harry?

Barker: I have an application form with me here.

Lil: [Disappointed.] Oh, ta.

Barker: Oh, and here's some chocolate. See you Monday!

[They sing:]

> Stretch a hand out across the sea
> I need you and you need me
> We shall save the economy
> If we become one big happy family
>
> Do your bit, join hands together
> Then together we can surely win the war
> Do your bit, join hands together
> I'll do my bit if you do yours.

[**Barker** goes. **Lil** is joined by **Annie**. Together they work on the production line.]

Lil: 'Ere Annie, what 'appens if something goes wrong on this line?

Annie: Don't ask me, gel. I just work 'ere.

Lil: I mean we've got procedure, 'ave we?

Annie: Procedure?

Lil: If someone's got a complaint. 'Oo'd we tell?

Annie: I dunno, love.

Lil: What your ol' man do?

Annie: Don't think they ever worked it out.

Lil: Just like men. All mouth an' no action. We ought a 'ave some representation in 'ere, darlin'. Just cos there's a bleedin' war on don't mean we got a put up with any old nonsense.

Annie: 'Ere 'ere.

Lil: Get the foreman over.

Annie: You can't do that, you'll get the sack!

31

Lil: Not me, gel. Essential Works Order, this is. If they try any thing on, I'll take it to Appeal. I know my rights, gel. — George! George!

George: [Timidly poking head round corner.] Er, yes?

Lil: 'Oo's our union representative in this 'ole?

George: Er well, love ... it's like this ... you ain't got one.

Lil: Ain't got one!

George: Well no, it's like ... non-union this place, en it?

Lil: Since when?

George: Well, like ... always. It's sort of never been sorted out.

Lil: Time it bleedin' was then. We want union representation in 'ere now, right?

George: Er, yeh well, all right.

Lil: Stop yer work, Annie. We're not workin' again till we get it. — All right, George?

George: Well, er ... I'll see what the guv'nor says, like.

Annie: An' we're sittin' down 'ere till we get it. — Got a fag, love — All right, George? You go off an' tell 'im.

George: Well, er ... yes. I will. — Er, Sir Merciful!

[**Sir Merciful Merry** appears, apart.]

Merry: Never fear, George. The word from Detroit is, we're all one big happy family. The unions, us and the national interest. The ladies can have what they want.

George: Yes, sir. [He goes to go back.]

Merry: Oh, but there's just one other thing, George.

George: Yes, sir?

Merry: I'm afraid we do have to negotiate directly with the TUC and the unions' national officers on this. No unseemly bar gaining or recruitment on the shop floor. Too much fraternis ation with the men's a bad thing, what. Labour's the unions business, the factory's Mr Big's. Got that?

George: Yes, sir. [He creeps back.]

Lil: All right, darlin', we 'eard. Least we know it's there now love, eh?

Annie: That's something.

Lil: Come on, let's get crackin'. We got a war to win.

[They go back to work, and sing:]

Women of the world unite
This is a battle everyone should fight
You can't ignore the economy
If you want a happy family

Do your bit, join hands together
Then together we can surely win the war

Do your bit, join hands together
I'll do my bit, if you do yours.

[**Harry** comes on with **Another Worker.**]

Harry: All right, my darlings, stand aside. The men are back from the war. Time to go home.

Annie: Home?

Harry: Back in the kitchen where you belong. I'll be wantin' me dinner in a couple of hours.

Lil: We been doin' as good as you. **You** go an' get the dinner. The apron's behind the door in the kitchen.

Worker: What sort of welcome's this then? We're yer conquerin' 'eroes.

Annie: Go an' conquer the spuds then.

Worker: I got a good mind to put you across my knee.

Annie: That may've gone down a treat with your French floosies, Jackie boy, but with me it's a lead balloon. Piss off.

George: Now let's keep it sweet please, no disruption. We got an order book long as your arm.

Harry: You keep out of this, George. This is family.

George: I'm sorry, it's orders. No argy-bargy. We got to rebuild England.

Worker: Blimey, same old song. Worse'n the bleedin' army.

Lil: I'll get the union.

Worker: Union?

Lil: Yeh. While you lot been on 'oliday we made a few improvements.

Harry: Where is it then? This union?

Lil: I put the address somewhere.

Annie: In your pocket.

Lil: No . . . I can't find it.

Harry: Never mind bits of paper, where's yer steward? No use 'avin' representation 'less it's in evidence. 'Ere on the shop floor.

George: I ain't 'avin' that!

Worker: Listen, George, you're talkin' to the blokes 'oo won the war for you.

George: But the Company don't allow shop stewards.

Harry: It may not allow 'em, sunshine, but it's gonn' a bleedin' get 'em. There's a Labour government in now, don't forget.

George: Sir Merciful won't like it.

Worker: 'E can get stuffed an' all. If 'e don't like it, we'll nationalise 'im. Tell 'im that from me.

George: I can't do that.

Harry: You refusin'?

George: Well, er . . . yes.

33

Harry: Right, that's it, girls. Everyone out. We'll celebrate the unio
with a strike.

Worker All out for the shop stewards! Down the pub!

George: But . . . but . . . what about the orders?

Harry: Sod 'em. I 'ad enough of them in the army!

[**The Workers** troop off 'round the pub', and sing:]

No more orders, we've had enough
Now it's their turn an' they can all get stuffed
We'll get our share of the economy
Now we're one big happy family

Do your bit, join hands together
Then together we can weather the storm
Do your bit, join hands together
I'll do my bit, if you do yours.

[**George** creeps back on.]

George: The boss says it's all right. You can 'ave your stewards.

Harry: Wised up at last, have they?

Worker Good old Clem Attlee!

George: So if you don't mind drinkin' up, lads . . . we can . . . er . . .
get back to, er . . . if you don't mind, that is.

Harry: Piss off, George, we've only just got 'ere. I'm not goin' back
till the others push the boat out an' all.

[They sing:]

The Union Song

We are united, united we stand
A formidable force in a trembling land
We are united, and we shall take power
We are the union, and the union is ours

We won't accept another empty promise
We won't be put off by excuses that they make
We'll get back all the things they've taken from us
We'll get back all the wealth that we create

We are united, united we stand
A formidable force, in a trembling land
We are united, and we shall take power
We are the union. The union is ours.

We have a world to win
The future is ours!

2.

1. The Peacetime Board-Room Ops Table

[**General, Chrysler, Big** and **The Guy Asleep Under Th**
Blanket. They sit round what was the pool table. It is no
an ops table with assets which they can push round on arm
Behind them a map of the world with pins and stickers

General: Peace at last, gentlemen! The war's over and here we a
again.

Chrysler: Peace throughout de woild! Peace for everyone!

Mr Big: Yeh. Dere's a piece for you, a piece for me an' a piece f
him.

General: Have a bit of decorum, will you?

Mr Big: What's wrong? Dere's enough for all of us. De woild ar
us. It's a cinch. It makes my mouth water just to look at
[To **Chrysler**] Which piece do you want. Chrysler? Sou
America? Shall I tell you what I fancy?

[**The Tea Lady** comes in with her trolley.]

Tea Lady: Tea?

[**Big** starts jumping up and down in excitement.]

Mr Big: Oh I can't make up my mind. Dere's so much of it! I
possibilities are endless! Oh boy! Oh boy!

Tea Lady: D'you mind not jumpin' up an' down like that, you're shaki
the cups.

Mr Big: It's too good to be true! It's too much! Oh boy!

Tea Lady: [To **Big**] I'm talkin' to you! — Like a little kid.

General: Quite right, lady. Pull yourself together, Big. Have a bit
respect for de lady's function in our new society we'
creatin', our big happy brotherhood of men.

Mr Big: Our what?

Tea Lady: One lump or two?

Mr Big: Three. — What are you talkin' about?

Tea Lady: Can't 'ave three, that's greedy.

Mr Big: You can't talk to me like dat! I'm de boss.

[**Tea Lady** puts the sugar down defiantly and crosses h
arms.]

General: Take two like de lady says, Big, or none of us gets any te
We gotta loin manners now. De old days is over. We gott

woik democratically like we did in de war. Moderation in all tings.

Mr Big: I'll take two.

[Satisfied, **The Tea Lady** gives him his sugar and goes.]

General: From now on we go legit. We're helpin' to make de rules so we gotta follow 'em. I'll take your weapons.

Mr Big: What?!

General: Guns we leave to de army. De guys makin' em's on our side so we don't gotta worry.

Chrysler: [Putting them on the table] One shot-gun, one .45, one knuckleduster, one stiletto.

General: [Doing the same.] Two pistols, a grenade an' a pick-axe. — Big?

Mr Big: Do I have to?

General: Go on!

Mr Big: A derringer, a flick-knife an' a phial of arsenic.

Chrysler: What about him?

General: Who?

Chrysler: De guy asleep under de blanket?

Mr Big: Yeh, he gives me de creeps.

General: Eah, leave him, he's harmless. — O.K., now that's over — [He clears the weapons away] — we can ask de guests in. Two gennulmen an' a lady well-known to you all who've been very useful to us over the last five years, an' to whom we owe a vast debt of gratitood: Uncle Sam, John Bull an' Mamsel Europa. I've invited 'em along outa de kindness of my heart, an' I wanna hear a big welcome for 'em.

Mr Big: Do we have to cut 'em in?

General: You don't loin, do you, dum-dum. Dey're harmless but we don't get nowhere widout deir co-operation. O.K., Chrysler, open de door. An' let's hear yer.

[**Chrysler** opens the door. **Hoods** sing a short anthem of praise and goodwill.]

> Thank-you, thank-you gennulmen
> Our thanks are due to you
> Thank-you, thank-you gennulmen
> And lady — thank-you too.

Uncle Sam: On behalf of us all, gentlemen, thank-you.

General: It's nuttin'. De least we can do. We're always happy to oblige.

Europa: As you did in ze war.

John Bull: Quite. We won the war . . .

Uncle Sam: We won the war . . .

General: . . . and we got our cash. It worked once, and it can work

	again. So we'd like to go on operating.
Europa:	Ze only difficulty is: 'ow do we know we can trust you?
John Bull:	Oh surely ... I mean, gentleman's agreement and all tha what?
Uncle Sam:	I know I'm a gent. I know you are. But how do I know he i [He indicates **Mr Big**.]

[Nasty pause.]

John Bull:	What one needs really is a standard.

[Pause.]

John Bull:	Something we all have faith in.

[Pause.]

John Bull:	Something with **sterling** quality.
Chrysler:	What you implyin', pal? There is no quality in sterlin any more.
Europa:	Yes, why not be franc?
General:	Dat's just as bad, lady. Our standard needs to be stronger than the pound or tl franc. It needs to have the experience of the war behind and behind that the experience of the depression at worst. A guarantee that will stand up to all kinds of drainir of its strength.

[They all look at **Uncle Sam**.]

Uncle Sam:	[Reluctantly fishing a dollar sign from his pocket.] OK, O I'll stand bail for you all. Only don't expect miracles. It just the dollar, that's all.
Mr Big:	Just the dollar, he says! Just the dollar!
General:	Do we all agree the dollar shall be our barometer?

[Nods and murmurs of agreement.]

Uncle Sam:	What about him? The guy under the blanket.
General:	He says he's from de Thoid Woild — whatever dat Forget him. He agrees with everything we say. He's got t
Chrysler:	That's terrific. No more depressions, our currencies stabilise cast-iron guarantees all round. No more problems.

[**The Tea Lady** pokes her head in.]

Tea Lady:	I suppose these three want tea now, do they?
John Bull:	Oh please.
General:	[Very polite.] If it's not too much trouble, Ma'am.
Tea Lady:	You should a said before, you know. [She brings in tea.]
General:	I know, I'm sorry, and I won't do it again.
Tea Lady:	Right. [She puts the cups down and goes.]

Uncle Sam: Just one thing, General. If I'm sticking my neck out for you guys, I have to know you're willing to keep the peace with the men in our countries who keep us all ticking over.

Mr Big: Who's he talking about?

Europa: Your labour force, Monsieur Big.

Mr Big: Oh. Is that important?

[They sing:]

Bretton Woods Song

Uncle Sam:
You are gentlemen now
And you've got to learn how
To behave like gentlemen do
If you put your trust in me
I'll put my trust in you

ll except Sam:
We agree to be as good as gold
The currencies we hold
We'll base against the dollar

Uncle Sam:
You are gentlemen now
And you've got to learn how
To behave just like gentlemen do
If you don't cheat on me
I won't cheat on you

All:
We agree to do the best we can
Thank-you Uncle Sam
Your monetary plan
Has stabilised our future

Uncle Sam: OK, the dollar stands. [He puts it on the table.] Look after it.

[**Griggs** bursts in, a heavy hood, out of breath, desperate.]

Griggs: You gotta help me, fellas, de situation's desperate. I'm on de run. [He sees **Uncle Sam.**] Oh, you're here.

Mr Big: Hiya, Griggsy!

Griggs: I must have de wrong office. [He goes to go.]

General: It's all right, Griggsy. We got an understanding with dese guys now.

Uncle Sam: What do you want, Griggs?

Griggs: I came to see de fellas about dis charge you got me on, Uncle Sam. I tell you, it's a frame-up.

General: What's de trouble, Griggsy?

Griggs: All I did was get involved in a little business wid a guy named Angelini an' it toins out de guy's a hood! ! Uncle Sam's got me on a charge of corruption. A two million dollar fine! Where do I find money like dat, fellas?

39

Mr Big: Say, Griggs. You got a plant near my motor works
Dagenham, England, ain't yer?

Griggs: Sure, Big. De body plant. Why?

Mr Big: I'll buy it off yer.

Griggs: How much?

Mr Big: Two million?

Griggs: [Disgusted.] Two . . . ! [He looks at **Uncle Sam.**] It's a d
[Pause. They all look at him.] Well, if you guys don't mi
I gotta go. [He nips off sharpish.]

John Bull: That means you've got two plants in Blighty now, Mr I
Next door to each other.

Mr Big: We been co-operating for a long time. [Realises what l
said.] — Not too close, mind.

[**Tea Lady** comes in with trolley.]

Tea Lady: Come on now, drink up, drink up. Some of us have
'omes to go to, you know.

[They hurriedly finish their tea as she clears up.]

Mr Big: Hey, we're gentlemen now. Can't we finish our tea ir
gentlemanly fashion?

Tea Lady: A real gentleman lets a lady get on with her work, Mr I

Mr Big: Something about dis lady reminds me. I'm gonna have to
something about the ungentlemanly elements in Griggs' bc
plant in England. If I gotta loin good manners, dey gotta t
What we need is a book of rules. Procedure.

2. The Griggs Plant, January 1957

[**Johnny McLoughlin** comes on through the audience, ringi
a handbell.]

McLoughlin: Meetin', brothers! All shop stewards in the River Pla
Meeting! Two shop stewards suspended! Everyone up
Jigs and Fixtures!

[**Another Steward** comes on.]

Steward: What's up, John?

McLoughlin: Two stewards suspended.

Steward: What for?

McLoughlin: What do you think? Doin' their job, that's all. We said we
meet if there were lay-offs, so that's what we're doin'.

Steward: Right.

McLoughlin: Meetin', meetin'! Shop Stewards Committee.

[**George the Foreman** comes running up.]

George: 'Ere, what's your game, John?

McLoughlin: I just been up the manager's office. 'E's suspended two of o

40

	blokes. We ain' 'avin' that. It's a meetin'.
George:	What d'you mean? You got no right. You're disruptin' the plant.
McLoughlin:	I ain't, the management is.
George:	Look, I'm warnin' you . . .
McLoughlin:	Leave it alone, George. Give yourself a rest.
George:	Right! [He storms off. By this time **The Other Stewards** have gathered.]
McLoughlin:	Right, lads. You'll remember in November the company announced that because of the Suez oil shortage they'd be layin' people off this January. It's January now, an' this is their way of doin' it. Two of our fellow stewards have been suspended. They're tryin' to break up our organisation. The thin end of the wedge. We have to protect ourselves against the management hirin' an' firin' as they please. Any suggestions?
2 Steward:	Get on to the branch, John.
3 Steward:	Get on to the national officials.
1 Steward:	Of all the unions.
2 Steward:	Just get crackin'.
McLoughlin:	Right.

[**George** comes back with **Manager**.]

George:	That's 'im, sir. Johnny McLoughlin. Went through the whole department, ringin' that bell. Causin' disruption, sir. These men've got work to do.
Manager:	What d'you have to say for yourself, McLoughlin?
McLoughlin:	We're not 'avin' our men laid off just like that.
Manager:	There's a time and place for any queries on management decisions.
McLoughlin:	That's right. Here an' now.
Manager:	I'm afraid not. You're paid to work in this plant, McLoughlin, not to disrupt the men.
McLoughlin:	We could wait till Doomsday for an answer from you lot.
3 Steward:	Or the union.
McLoughlin:	Once a man's outside the gate, 'e's 'ad it.
Manager:	I'm afraid I must ask you to call this meeting off.
McLoughlin:	Lads?
1 Steward:	No chance.

[**The Others** agree.]

McLoughlin:	That's your answer.
Manager:	In that case you can join your friends outside, McLoughlin. Collect your cards from Personnel.

[**The Manager** and **George** go.]

1 Steward:	I ain't puttin' up with this. One out, all out, I reckon.
2 Steward:	Dead right. You, Len?
3 Steward:	I'm ready.
1 Steward:	Right then, call your lads together an' we'll take a vote

[They walk out.]

Mr Big:	[**Mr Big** alone at his ops table, on the phone.] What do mean they just walked out? Who do they think they are? [Calmer.] Sorry. I let my feelings run away with me. V ungentlemanly. — So what do we do? — Find a gentlema solution. Get an expert in. Someone rational, some objective. Yeh, that's it, a university man. Preferably fr one receivin' support from the Big Foundation. — No, course he should be impartial! — A Lord would be fine. always found them reliable in the past. — Scottish? Go They never give anything away.

[**Lord Macaroon,** donnish, comes in.]

Macaroon:	Lord Macaroon at your service.
Mr Big:	I've got a problem, Macaroon. Ungentlemanly elements the shop floor.
Macaroon:	Ah. Breakdown of civilisation. Rome, the Incas. Resurge of barbaric instincts, that sort of thing?
Mr Big:	They're on strike.
Macaroon:	Ah. Refusal to work. Spartacus. The Animal within M
Mr Big:	You got it: animals! Shop stewards leadin' the men wreckin' production.
Macaroon:	Of course. Leaders and the led. Abuse of authority. Po without responsibility.
Mr Big:	We gotta get 'em back to work.
Macaroon:	Restoration of status quo. Re-establish natural balan Harmony of conflict.
Mr Big:	I think it's the Communist influence.
Macaroon:	Foreign, Jewish philosophy. Translates very badly i English.
Mr Big:	You got the job.
Macaroon:	Good, well, get 'em back to work and we'll sort it out
Mr Big:	Get 'em workin' **before** your report?
Macaroon:	This is an Inquiry into Labour problems, isn't it? If they not labouring, we've got nothing to inquire into. That's w reports of this kind are all about. McLoughlin! [He ta up a pulpit-like position. **McLoughlin** comes on opposite h He chants his verdict.]
	I define: you, John McLoughlin as an unruly element and your demeanour as glib, quick-witted a evasive.

Macaroon: I define: you as a man not worried about his job or the effects of his actions

and as showing a considerable capacity for agitation and propaganda.

This being so,

I define: the Big Motor Company's decision to dismiss you as totally justified.

and its right to manage as incontrovertible.

Finally,

I define: the presence of Communist influence in Shop Steward committees as undesirable

and the continued existence of such uncontrolled committees as in nobody's interest.

Mr Big: Not in mine, not in the Government's, not in the unions'. Only in the workers'. Procedure? I like it.

3. Procedure, 1958

[**George the Foreman** counting seconds on a stop watch, mumbling to himself.]

George: 508, 509, 510, 511 — I'm not 'avin' any more a this shirkin'. 10, 12, 15 minutes for tea-break? Nine minutes it should be, and no more! — 520, 521, 522 — General Foreman breathin' down me neck all the time, 'intin' at shake-ups. I'm not gettin' shaken up — or moved 'sideways'. There's only one direction sideways an' that's out. — 538, 539, 540! Right, that's it, nine minutes. All present and correct? No! 'Oo's missin'? Reynolds. All right Reynolds, I've got you this time. [**Reynolds** comes on.] Eight 'n' arf seconds late! Eight point five! D'you 'ear that?

Reynolds: 'Oo me?

George: Yes! Easy George they used to call me. No more! You're eight 'n' arf seconds late. Eight 'n' arf seconds of company time!

Reynolds: Look, George, I only went ...

George: I don't wan' a know!

Reynolds: Me zip got stuck!

[**George** involuntarily punches him in the face.]

Reynolds: 'Ere, you 'it me!

George: Oh. — Er, I'm not 'avin' it. Other foremen laughin' at me. You been takin' advantage.

Reynolds: You better apologise for that, George.

George: No! I'm gettin' 'ard now, Reynolds, I'm a foreman. Go⟨ be'ave like a foreman.

Reynolds: That case I'm goin' a 'ave t' give yer one back.

George: Now look 'ere . . . !

Reynolds: Where d'you wan' it?

George: You can't 'it me. It's in 'ere, the Blue Book. Procedu⟨ 'Disorderly conduct on the Company's premises, regarded dangerous and forbidden.'

Reynolds: Where's it say that? [He looks at his own copy.]

George: Page 136. This is you, look: injury. 'If you are injured in ⟨ accident at work, advise your Supervisor immediately a⟨ report to First Aid.'

Reynolds: Thass no good, it weren't an accident. You did it delibera⟨ Whass it say about foremen? — Nothin'. 'Ittin'? — N⟨ Grievous bodily 'arm p'raps — Ah! 'Grievance Procedu⟨ Page 11. '— 'Any employee 'oo wishes t' raise any matt⟨ shall first discuss it with 'is . . . foreman.' Foreman?!

George: Yes, son? What's the trouble?

Reynolds: [Reading.] 'The foreman must give a reply within a max⟨ mum of two workin' shifts.' — Well? What's yer reply?

Foreman: Work two shifts an' I'll tell yer.

Reynolds: Right! [He whistles, goes over to a calendar and rips tw⟨ pages off. **George comes back.**] Right, two days is up. Y⟨ 'it me!

George: I didn't! When was that? [He goes.]

Reynolds: [Reading.] 'If the employee is not satisfied, 'e may discu⟨ the matter with 'is shop steward, an' t'gether they may ma⟨ a further approach to the Foreman.' — Oh no! — Oh. ⟨ 'And/or General Foreman.' Great! Danny!

[**Danny, the Shop Steward,** appears immediately.]

Danny: Yes, son?

Reynolds: George 'it me. I wan' a take it to the General Foreman.

Danny: Right. — Charlie!

Charlie: [Appearing immediately.] 'Allo.

Reynolds: George 'it me.

Charlie: I'm a bit busy now, fellas. See me the day after the d⟨ after tomorrow. [He goes.]

Reynolds: [Reading.] "Oo must reply within a maximum of three wor⟨ in' shifts.' Right. [He and **Danny** whistle, rip off three da⟨ on the calendar. **Charlie** and **George** come past.] Right! Three days is past. 'E 'it me!

Charlie: Did you, George?

George: I don't remember. Couldn't 'ave been 'ard if I did.

Charlie: 'Ow 'ard couldn't it 'ave been, d'you reckon?

44

George: 'Bout this 'ard? [He bashes **Reynolds** again.]

Reynolds: Oi! [To **Danny**] There, look. 'E did it again.

Charlie: No. 'E was just showin' you 'ow 'e didn't do it. [He and **George** go.]

Reynolds: [Reading.] 'If there is still no satisfaction, raise the matter with the appropriate superintendent.'

Danny: Tom!

Super: [Appearing immediately.] Mornin'.

Danny: One of your foremen punched this lad 'ere on the nose.

Super: Look, I'm just going off for the weekend. Can't it wait till next week? [He goes.]

Reynolds: [Reading.] ''Oo must reply within five workin' shifts.' Right. [He and **Danny** whistle. Rip off five days on the calendar. **Superintendent, Charlie** and **George** come past.]

Danny: Right. Five shifts are over. What about this punch-up?

Super: What punch-up?

George: Reynolds claims I punched 'im on the nose.

Super: How d'you mean?

George: Like this. [He punches **Reynolds** again.]

Super: Did you?

George: No. It was more like this. [He punches **Reynolds** again and goes off with **Superintendent.**]

Reynolds: [Reading.] 'If no satisfaction has been reached, refer the matter within seven days to the Personnel Manager.'

Danny: Watkins!

Reynolds: 'Ere 'ang on, I go on 'oliday t'morrer. [They stand whistling and ripping off 14 days on the calendar. **George** and **The Personnel Manager** come past.]

Now look 'ere, I've 'ad enough of this. Very simple complaint. 'E bopped me one. Bunch of fives, knuckle sandwich. 'E's off 'is rocker, losin' 'is marbles cos 'e thinks 'es for the boot.

George: 'Oo is?

Reynolds: You!

[**George** hits **Reynolds** again.]

Danny: There are! 'E did it again!

Personnel: Provocation. He insulted him.

Reynolds: It weren't provoked before, though.

Personnel: What d'you mean?

Reynolds: It was unprovoked.

George: [Hitting him.] Like that, you mean?

Reynolds: Yeh, that's more like it. — 'Ere!

[**George** backs off, fearing retaliation.]

Personnel: Surely he couldn't have hit you from that distance.

Reynolds: No, he was nearer. Like just now.

George: No I wasn't. It was you 'oo was nearer.

Reynolds: All right, I was nearer! [He moves up to **George**, who h him.]

George: That's about the distance, yes.

Personnel: Good, that's settled then. [He goes.]

Reynolds: This is ridiculous. I'm gettin' punch-drunk. [He read 'If not then resolved, Labour Relations Manager.'

Danny: Mr Phillips!

Phillips: [Appearing immediately.] Yes?

George: 'Allo, Dad. [**Phillips** goes.]

Reynolds: 'If not then resolved, bring in the union and the Jo Negotiating Committee.'

Danny: Vic!

Vic: [Appearing immediately.] Mornin', brothers.

Danny: You've 'eard about this lad, 'ave you?

Vic: Aye, brother. No problem. Leave it to me.

Reynolds: Ah! Someone talkin' sense at last.

Vic: The way I see it, 'e poonched you, right?

Reynolds: That's it! On the nail! You got it!

Vic: Right. Poonch 'im back then.

Reynolds: Great! [He punches **George**.]

George: 'Ere! [He punches **Reynolds**.]

Reynolds: 'E did it again! RIGHT!! [He rolls his sleeves up fo proper fight.]

Vic: Now, now brother. Unconstitutional.

Reynolds: Wha-?

Vic: If you've got a complaint, you 'ave t'go through procedu Stage One: take the matter oop with your foreman.

Reynolds: Oh no! [**George** goes, well-satisfied.] I was only eight 'n ' seconds late ... I got me zip stuck ... I'll never go for a p again. Never!

Vic: 'Ere are, lad. 'Ave this.

Reynolds: What's that?

Vic: Yer gold watch. You'll be about due fer it, time you through.

Reynolds: I'm not goin' a be beaten. I got a get a grip on meself. Car on like this, I'll end up in Barley Lane.

Vic: If you take my advice, son, you'll forget about it. What y need's cheerin' oop. Tekkin' out o' yersen. Get away fr it all. Buy yersen a little car.

Reynolds: You reckon?

Vic: Aye. After all, you've never 'ad it so good, as Macmill never tires of tellin' oos.

Reynolds: The fruits of me labour. Right, I'll do that. Thank you.

[Scene breaks. **Vic** goes off. **Reynolds** walks into:]

4. The Consumer, 1960

[Ting! Sound effect as **Reynolds** either walks thro' door or summons **Assistant,** who comes immediately.]

Assistant: Good morning, sir. Can I help you, be of any assistance, talk you into anything?

Reynolds: I wan' a buy a car.

Assistant: Up and away, eh sir? Live dangerously. That the sort of thing?

Reynolds: Not too dangerously.

Assistant: But thrust, power, style.

Reynolds: Yeh, that's it.

Assistant: Then you need the new Big Concertina. The car for the man who is a man. Sporty, fast, a car to love 'em an' leave 'em in.

Reynolds: Oh yes?

Assistant: Make those week-ends away a real pleasure, if you know what I mean, sir.

Reynolds: Say n'more.

Assistant: You'll be fighting them off. Stopping in lay-bys as they thumb lifts on the motorway, showing off their legs. You'll get hours of fun out of it.

Reynolds: Yes?

Assistant: Reclining seat so you don't wear your trouser-knees out.

Reynolds: Really?

Assistant: Also superb acceleration for the quick getaway. Here today and gone tomorrow.

Reynolds: That's the sort of thing.

Assistant: Glove compartment for the ... er ... bubble-gum.

Reynolds: Aha! Yes.

Assistant: An absolute bargain. At the price we're giving them away.

Reynolds: Er yes, how much is it exactly?

Assistant: Price is no object. Not to a man of your calibre. I can tell that without looking at you.

[Ting! **Reynolds' Wife** comes into the shop.]

Wife: I thought I'd find you here.

Reynolds: [Apologetic, to **Salesman.**] My wife.

Wife: Just as well I did. [To **Salesman.**] God knows what he'd finish up with if I wasn't around to help him.

Assistant: Well quite. Clearly what you need is a car to please both of you. For the family. Sturdy, reliable, safe. Economic to run, plenty of room for the kiddies. The car you know will start on cold mornings and keep you in sickness and in health, richer or poorer, for better or worse. Week-end picnics, reclining seat for mother-in-law's lumbago, a glove com-

Assistant: partment where you can keep . . .

Reynolds: No!

Assistant: . . tissues for the kiddies' sticky fingers.

Reynolds: Yeh well, I'm not sure . . .

Wife: No, it sounds nice.

Assistant: Then the Concertina is the car for you.

Reynolds: The same car?

Assistant: The Universal car, sir, for the modest family budget. I
last you all the way home for a mere £800.

Reynolds: Is that the only one you have?

Assistant: We sold 500,000 of them last year, sir.

Reynolds: So Bigs sell 400 million pounds worth of cars a year.

Assistant: Something like that.

Reynolds: And there's 50,000 of us working for the company, so we
personally make 10 cars a year.

Assistant: [Horrified] You make the car, sir? [Recovering] Then you
know all about its quality.

Reynolds: Not 'arf.

Assistant: And you must be a wealthy man. The British public know
all about you car-workers, mmm?

Reynolds: Look, on my wages I could just about afford one of these
year. How come I make 10 and can afford only one?

Assistant: Is that a riddle, sir?

Wife: Sounds more like a fiddle.

Assistant: You've got to remember the overheads, sir. [He goes.]

Reynolds: Overheads or no overheads, they're makin' 20 pounds a we
out of me — and it's goin' out a the country. 'Oo's gettin' t
other nine cars? That's what I wan' a know!

Reynolds & Wife: [Sing :]

There are thieves in the factories
Who never get found out
They profit from our labour
That's what business is about

They profit from our wage — they pass it on
They take the goods we make — they pass it on
They pass it on and on and on until it stops
In the shops

First we lose in the factories
Then we lose in the shops
Count your wages carefully
Calculate the cost

They profit from our wage — they pass it on, etc.

The day they realised
That theft was legalised
Ah what a paradise
This world became for thieves

They profit from our wage — they pass it on, etc.

[They go off.]

5. Mr Big calls on Pappy in Triumph

[**Mr Big,** at his table, playing with several model cars.]

Mr Big: Vrrm, vrrm! One for you, nine for me. Vrrrrrrrrmmm! Yep, profits by the million again last year, Pappy, and my workers can afford to buy the cars I make. My dream's come true!

Pappy: So what d'you want me for, son?

Mr Big: I just wanted you to admit I was right, Pappy. We've none of us had it so good!

Pappy: Don't trust it, eh son?

Mr Big: What d'yer mean?

Pappy: Too good to be true? You only come to me in times of difficulty. There's gotta be somethin' worryin' yer.

Mr Big: How long's the dream gonna last, Pappy? For ever?

Pappy: Sorry to disappoint you, son, but this is just an Indian summer you're enjoying now. Have you checked Uncle Sam's barometer?

Mr Big: It says changeable. But that's ridiculous. There ain't a cloud in the sky.

Pappy: Make hay while the sun shines, son. There'll be a storm blowin' up before long.

Mr Big: Oh Pa, that's nonsense. See for yourself. Vrrm! Vrrm!

Pappy: Still fightin' the same problem you always were, son?

Mr Big: An' beatin' it.

Pappy: For the moment, yes. You've learnt to diversify, yer're sittin' on top of the world an' it's one big market for yer. Trouble is, when the weather's fine, everyone wants to be a farmer. Them new markets sure is gettin' crowded.

Mr Big: That's all right, Pa, we've got new rules now, we're gentlemen farmers. Anyway they're all small fry in the new markets.

Pappy: You were small fry once too, son. An' they're all gonna want to store in their barns just like you did. 'Sides, the places all you farmers is deprivin' is gittin' poorer an' poorer. One day they'll twig what's happenin' an' keep for themselves what you want.

Mr Big: What in tarnation you talkin' about, Pappy?

Pappy: 'S oil, son. 'S oil.

Mr Big: Goddamit, Pappy, I keep tellin' yer, I ain't a farmer.

Pappy: Yer're not listenin' carefully, son. I tell yer yer problem. I' oil.

Mr Big: It's nothing to do with soil, Pappy. I make motor cars.

Pappy: Well, you won't listen an' I'm losin' my beauty sleep.

Mr Big: I don't ever wanna hear you again, Pappy. You're stupid a misleadin'. It's goodbye for ever this time. Goodbye!

Pappy: Goodbye, son.

6. The Gym

[**Tommy Toyota** comes on with a great cry and a kara leap, then does exercises. **Johann Volkswagen** comes c goose-stepping with weights on his feet and arms. **Dino Fi** and **Charles De Renault** come on together with a 'test you strength' machine, then box together. Each of them has h name written large on his back. They do various exercis throughout the scene. As these work out. **The Guy Aslee Under The Blanket** slips in unnoticed and settles down i a corner.]

Toyota: Honoulable Johann looking velly fit these days.

VW: [With chest expanders.] Jawohl. Our chests are expandin every day, you know.

Toyota: Ours too. Gleat advantage in being smashed to pieces i war.

VW: Jawohl! Vunce ve got ofer ze pain off doink ze splits, w realised ve het to rebuild our crippled industries.

Renault: An' now 'e 'as biceps like tree-trunks, hein?

VW: You too cen hef a body like mine.

Renault: Eef I'm not careful, hein?

Toyota: Mr Big teach lesson of find new markets. New machine: new factories an' plenty investment flom Uncle Sam Japanese learn velly fast. Income lises, more plofits. Vell healthy. Yahay! [He karates something.]

Renault: Not too deeficul' when you 'ave so much cheap labour, hein

Toyota: Uncle Sam only invest in machines. Not men. And when h do invest in men, only small.

Fiat: Why'sa data?

Toyota: Only small men. Yahay! [He karates something else.]

Renault: Ze Italian also is not noted for ees size, eh Dino?

VW: Nor his discipline!

Toyota: Velly solly you got that kind ploblems, Dino.

VW: Vot he needs is unions like mine. Ve made zem ourselves Ha!

Renault: Democratic labour relations, 'e calls zem. Workaires wiz shares in ze factoree. Workaires' councils on ze boards of directors. Every workaire becomes a capitalist! Not bad! You should try zat, Dino.

Fiat: Why bother? Mya peasantsa froma the Southa worka fora peanuts.

VW: Like my immigrants.

Renault: And what does 'e do? Ze guy undaire ze blankette?

Fiat: Hea sleeps alla day. A sevena stone weakiling! The Third World. Underdeveloped.

[**Mr Big** bursts in, college-boy athlete.]

Mr Big: Hi there, fellas! [**The Four** shout their greetings.] Workin' out hard, huh? That's what I like to see. Prosperity and happiness can only be obtained through honest effort. I guess you guys are glad you took up my training methods, huh?

Fiat: Surea thing, Mr Big.

VW: Jawohl.

[**Others** murmur their assent.]

Mr Big: Well, carry on the way you're going and you'll all do very well for yourselves.

Toyota: One day get as big as Mr Big himself, eh?

Mr Big: [Laughing] Well, I guess you'll have to work out pretty hard to do that, Toyota. Specially with those strange exercises of yours. What do you call that?

Toyota: Kung Fu.

Mr Big: Nice with noodles, huh? [**Renault** and **Fiat** have stopped working out.] Come on, you two, no slacking! You'll never get anywhere less you keep at it.

[**Renault** and **Fiat** box in a desultory way.]

Mr Big: Jees, you guys just don't know what's good for you, do you. [He goes up to the 'test your strength' machine and blows a whistle. Everything stops.] Every day for twenty years — ever since the war — I've come here, done a few exercises to keep in trim and rung the bell on this machine without fail. A sound constitution, boys, makes for a healthy people. [He bashes the machine. Nothing happens. Everyone stops. Silence. He bashes it again. Nothing.] Must be something wrong with the goddam machine. [He bashes it again. Nothing.]

Toyota: Let me tly.

Mr Big: Come on now, Toyota, you tryin' to tell me if I can't ring

51

the bell, a little fella like you can? [He laughs.] Machin
bust, that's all.

Toyota: If Honoulable Big permit: Yahay! [He karates the machi
It rings.] Number one lesson: cheap labour. Velly glatef
master. [He goes.]

VW: [Stepping up.] Scuse please. Ooovay! [He rings the bel
Second lesson: social democracy. Danke schön. [He goe

[**Fiat** and **Renault** come up together. Their combined fi
ring the bell.]

Renault: Leçon trois: **United** States, Economic Community. Mer
monsieur. [He and **Fiat** go, taking the machine with ther

Mr Big: [Alone] Pappy! — No, goddamit, I don't need him. J
got to work out a bit harder, that's all. On the shop flo
That's where the trouble is.

7. The Victimisation of the Seventeen, 1962

Foreman's Song

[Sings:]

Nobody loves the foreman
This job is a bleedin' dead loss
Nobody loves the foreman
Not even the foreman's boss

He has a go at me
He shouts and then he moans at me
When things go wrong
The foreman is just someone to be
Pissed upon

When I was ordinary worker
Life was hard but life made sense
Since I became a foreman
I've been sitting on the fence

This job would drive you mad
It's hard to understand
Whose side you're on
The foreman is just someone to be
Pissed upon

Nobody loves the foreman
It's a miserable kind of life
Nobody loves the foreman
Not even the foreman's wife

She's never satisfied
Although she knows how hard I tried
To get along
She thinks a foreman's just someone to be
Pissed upon

[**Five Workers** clock on and take up positions on the carousel. Natural faces become robotised. They mime the job they perform.]

Worker 1: Where's Terry this morning?

Worker 2: Been moved off.

Worker 3: Can't trust 'em, can you.

Worker 1: What d'you mean?

Worker 3: When they increased the work-load from 32 parts to 35, we agreed on condition there was no more increases after that.

Worker 4: You mean, they're speedin' up again?

Worker 3: Taken a man off. It's the same thing. Each of us is producing four more parts a shift.

Worker 5: Christ! It's 'ard enough to keep up with it as it is.

Worker 3: Right. They're only happy if we're doin' the impossible.

Worker 5: You learn to cope with one rate, then they increase it.

Worker 2: Far as the company's concerned, lad, that's your fault for bein' new.

Worker 3: You learn to cope with it, so you've got a bit of dignity doin' it; you're masterin' the machine, not it masterin' you; you earn yourself a few seconds break every so often, then they decide if you're not sweatin' yer bollocks off, they must be able to get more work out of you.

Worker 5: It's no good, I'm goin'! [He gets out of rhythm and collides with **First Worker.**]

Worker 2: What's the matter?

Worker 1: 'E's fallin' behind.

Worker 2: If you can't keep up, son, miss every one in four. That's the extra they bunged on us. We'll all do the same. Rather than bugger the lot, which is what they deserve.

Worker 5: Right.

[**Shop Steward Bill** passes.]

Worker 2: Christ, I can 'ardly keep up myself. — Bill!

Bill: Mornin'. Goin' all right?

Worker 2: No it bloody ain't!

Worker 4: They took a man off. — Oh Christ. [He falls behind.]

Worker 3: Leave it.

[**George The Foreman** comes on.]

George: Whass goin' on 'ere?

Worker 3: It's the increased work-load. We can't cope.

George: It's the same rate.

Worker 3: Not quite. You took a man off. Remember?

George: So?

Worker 3: So we got four more parts per shift to get through.

George: Right little mathematician we got 'ere. Did you call 'im
[He indicates **Bill.**]

Worker 3: 'E was passin', thass all.

Bill: You ought to get the other man back on, George.

George: Well, you're not doin' nothin', are you. You step in. G
'em a hand.

Bill: They'll still need their other man, George. I'll step in
now if you go an' tell the Superintendent.

George: 'E won't 'ave it, I'm tellin' you.

Bill: We've shown good will. You go an' tell 'im.

George: All right. [He goes. **Bill** steps into the line.]

Bill: This is no bleedin' good, is it.

Worker 3: It's dishonest. Like stealin'. Rippin' off our time, energy
dignity just to squeeze another four lousy parts out. T
suggestion behind it is, we're fuckin' slack.

Bill: They're askin' for a show-down. This bloody speed-u
been goin' on everywhere. You think they'd 'ave more se
They lost 200,000 man-hours last year through stoppa
It'll be double that this year if they go on like this.

[**George** comes back with **Sixth Worker.**]

Worker 3: 'Oo-bleedin'-ray. Seen a bit of sense at last, have they?

[**Bill** comes out of the line.]

Worker 2: From the labour pool, is he?

George: That's right.

Worker 3: If we're gettin' the other bloke back, why can't we
Terry? 'E knew the job.

George: [To **3 Worker**] You out. [To **6 Worker**] Take over, s

[**6 Worker** steps into the line.]

Worker 3: 'Ere, whass the game?

Bill: What you up to, George?

George: 'E's not an extra man, 'e's a replacement. The Comp
won't 'ave people leadin' resistance to increased product

Worker 3: 'Leadin' resistance?' That's a joke.

Bill: The resistance is in their muscles, George. These blokes
like wet rags when they get 'ome.

[**6 Worker** falls behind. The line breaks down.]

Worker 4: Right, that's it. I've 'ad enough.

Worker 1: An' me.

Worker 2: Put Johnny back, George, or we're all stoppin'.

George: You tellin' me what to do?

Bill: It makes sense, George. The line's not workin', is it.

George: All right, get back on it. [3 **Worker** goes back on the line. 6 **Worker** comes off.] I'll see what management says. [He goes to a phone.]

Worker 2: What's he playin' at, Bill? Can't they see it won't work?

Bill: Not from where they're sittin'.

Worker 2: 'Ang on till 'e's finished on the phone. I don't trust that lot.

Bill: If they think you're resistin' production, they'll try an' get 'ard.

Worker 2: You reckon?

Bill: Don't wanna lose face, do they.

[**George** comes back.]

Bill: Well?

George: 'E's got a come off. — Take over, son. [6 **Worker**.]

Worker 4: Where's Johnny goin'?

George: We're movin' 'im somewhere else.

[**All Five Workers** stop.]

Worker 2: We're not 'avin' that.

Bill: [To **George**] Get on the phone an' tell 'em I wan' a talk to 'em.

George: All right, look. Johnny stays 'ere for now, but the line's got a keep movin', an' that lad's [6 **Worker**] got a be doin' the work. Otherwise **I'm** in trouble.

Bill: All right, let's get on that phone. [He and **George** go to the phone.]

Worker 5: What kind of joke is this? This ain't solvin' nothin'.

Worker 1: All right for them, sittin' in their offices, movin' men about. Takes a man time to learn this job.

Worker 6: No bleedin' picnic for me neither.

Worker 1: Right you are son. 'Ow can 'e [6 **Worker**] do 'is quota till 'e's learned the job?

Worker 4: On paper a job's just a job, en it. Just another function to make things balance on the bleedin' paper.

[**Bill** and **George** come back.]

Bill: I explained the position to 'em, lads. The answer I got was, the 'ole line'll be shut down if you keep fallin' behind.

Worker 3: What sort of answer's that? They didn't even 'ear the bloody question!

55

Bill: I told 'em the result of puttin' a replacement in was t
the 'ole line was disrupted, an' asked for Johnny to be
back. They refused that.

Worker 4: What kind a morons, are they, then?

Bill: I told 'em if they was thinkin' of shuttin' the line down, t
were obliged to go through procedure.

Worker 2: Right. Once we're locked outside the gates, they can
what they like.

Bill: Right. So I asked for a Joint Works Committee.

Worker 2: And?

Bill: They more or less said we could whistle for it.

Worker 3: So?

Bill: I told 'em no action till district officials were called in

Worker 3: And?

Bill: Refused. [The hooter sounds.] All right, before you go
for lunch, we better talk this over. [To **George** who's
standing there:] What do you want?

George: Nothing. [He goes.]

Bill: The problem is, what action do we take if they repl
Johnny permanently or shut the line down and lock pe
out.

Worker 1: Well, we're all in it together, en't we. Even the blokes fur
down the line. If we fall behind, it affects them. Be
same thing if one of their blokes was taken off.

Bill: Right.

Worker 2: If there's any action of that sort we're all together. N
strike.

Bill: All right. You know where to find me. [He goes.]

[Hooter. The men re-start. As they work, they sing:]

The Carousel Song

The Carousel turns round, around it goes
We stand in line
We spend our time
(We stand in line, we spend our time)
We watch the wheels wind

And a man turns around, around he goes
There's never time
For him to find
(There's never time for him to find)
A little peace of mind

And the world turns around, around it goes
It seems to me
Machinery's

56

General: [To **Barker**] Wise guy, huh?

Mr Big: Mind if I join the game?

General: Sure help yourself.

Mr Big: What do I do?

General: Well, dere ain't much left, but you try hittin' dese balls w de numbers on into dese pockets.

Mr Big: Like this?

Chrysler: Only you gotta hit dis ball foist.

Mr Big: Oh I get it. Not very efficient, but still . . . [He plays a sho R-r-rip.] Gee, fellas, sorry.

Chrysler: Forget it, we're gettin' a bigger table anyway. [He takes t cue and starts lining up a shot.]

Mr Big: Er, say fellas, this may not be a good time to bring t subject up, but, er, the racket in this town's been gettin' little hard just lately. Difficult to make ends meet.

General: I hadn't noticed.

[**Chrysler** plays a shot.]

Mr Big: You know: markets collapsin', the boys gangin' togethe stuff like that.

General: I don't recall nuttin'.

Chrysler: If de boys want more, give it to 'em, dey got a right. [H plays a shot.]

Mr Big: I was just thinking maybe we should come to some agre ment. This town's big enough for all of us. We don't have give each other aggravation.

General: Each to his own little precinct, huh?

Mr Big: Sure, that's right, you got it.

General: Fine. You do that.

Mr Big: That way no-one gets hurt.

Chrysler: You're a real gentleman, Big. [He plays his last shot. F and **General** start to walk off.]

Mr Big: Er, the other thing is, fellas, if you've got a minute, I'd li to learn this game.

General: No time, Big, sorry.

Chrysler: We'd like to help you, old-timer, but you know how it business calls.

[They go. **Barker** starts playing with a coin.]

Mr Big: Er, fellas . . .! They've gone. You see what I have to p up with, Barker. These guys are hoodlums. Hoods. Su people have no place in the motor trade.

Barker: If you're not careful, Mr Big, they'll have **your** place.

Mr Big: What can I do, Barker?

Barker: [Manipulating the coin like a gangster] Loin de game.

14

> (It seems to me machinery's)
> A part of me
>
> And then a day goes by, and then a week
> Another day another week and then a year is lost
> What a way to spend a day to
> Spend a week and no-one speaks of all the dreams
>   that stopped!
>
> Just come inside and take a ride!

[The men stop. During the song **George** has come on.]

George: Bill Francis, you're dismissed. Holdin' a meetin' on the premises durin' lunch.

[**The Workers** walk out, leaving **George** on his own. At his ops table **Mr Big** is on the phone.]

Mr Big: Get 'em back in there. We've lost 300,000 man-hours already this year. — I don't care, promise 'em anything. — Yeh, no victimisation, and we'll negotiate over this shop steward, this Bill Francis character. — We'll step up production over a week and let them back in gradually as we do. — Sure. They'll all be back working by the end of the week. There might be normal redundancies of course ... — Oh one thing. I'm going to get a letter out to them. As they go back, they've got to sign a pledge of good behaviour. A gentleman's agreement. — Yeh, good idea. Move 'em around. I don't want this trouble repeated.

[Hooter again. **The Workers** come back, with their letters. **George The Foreman** checks their letters and gets them to sign their pledge. In return he gives them a halo each, which they wear as, angelically, they return to the line.]

George: ... OK, sign here. [He gives **1 Worker** his halo. **The Worker** goes to go.] No, not that way. We've moved you to a different job. The speed's 40 a shift.

Worker 1: How do I know that?

George: Don't get stroppy, son. There's still hundreds outside the gates, remember.

Worker 1: Jesus, what is this? [He takes his place with the others. There are only four. **The Third Worker is missing.**] Where's Johnny?

Worker 2: No sign of him.

Worker 4: They're weedin' out the militants, that's what.

Worker 2: 600 still left outside.

Worker 4: An' they promised no victimisation!

Worker 5: If they've left Johnny outside, what chance Bill Franc‹ gettin' back in?

George: What's the trouble?

Worker 1: Why ain't Johnny back?

George: They asked us for lists of unsatisfactory employees.

Worker 5: What's unsatisfactory about Johnny? I'm the weak li‹ on this team.

George: You keep your mouth shut though. Good idea in t‹ circumstances.

[Hooter.]

Mr Big: A cut in poichase tax? That means cheaper cars, more sal‹ We need more men in there — leave only the woist out. ‹ can't afford to get left behind. Otherwise it's woiking we‹

[Hooter. **3 Worker** comes on, with letter.]

George: Sign here. [He gives **3 Worker** his halo.]

Worker 4: Over here, Johnny! — Whass goin' on?

Worker 3: Seventeen still left outside, includin' Bill Francis. All mi‹ tants, all shop stewards.

Worker 1: What is this?

Worker 3: 'They concluded over a period these were not men wi‹ goodwill towards the company.'

[Pause.]

Worker 4: 'Oo is?

8. Laugh Along with Uncle Sam and John Bul‹

John Bull: [Coming on.] I say, I say, I say. Talking of goodwill, ha‹ you made yours out yet, Uncle Sam?

Uncle Sam: Made what out, John Bull?

John Bull: Your will.

Uncle Sam: I won't.

John Bull: You won't what?

Uncle Sam: Leave you any.

John Bull: Oh how mean! I'm crushed! Desolated!

Uncle Sam: The whole world against you, huh?

John Bull: You should know. You own most of it.

Uncle Sam: I'm keeping it safe for democracy.

John Bull: Ah yes, Vietnam. Never mind, the war will soon be over.

Uncle Sam: Over? D'you think so?

John Bull: Over into Cambodia! Anyone for dominoes?!

Uncle Sam: You guys don't appreciate what I'm doing for you.

58

John Bull: I did my share once though, Uncle Sam. What's red and never sinks?

Uncle Sam: I don't know.

John Bull: The sun on the British Empire!

Uncle Sam: You got a long memory, John Bull. What's green and never rises?

John Bull: The pound?

Uncle Sam: You got it.

John Bull: No I haven't. That's why I came to see you. I want a loan.

Uncle Sam: You're not alone. Everyone wants one.

John Bull: But what about the gentleman's agreement? Bretton Woods?

Uncle Sam: Some gentleman! My dollar's supposed to be as good as gold. I put it into Vietnam, into Europe, into foreign aid. What do they do? Change it back into gold. Don't they trust my dollar?

John Bull: Never mind, Uncle Sam. Somebody still loves your dollar.

Uncle Sam: Who?

John Bull: Give us a long term loan and I'll tell you. [He purses his lips: 'kiss-kiss'.]

Uncle Sam: You've got as inflated an ego as the rest of them. There's no substance behind any of you. Suddenly the whole world's printing money.

John Bull: Print me some.

Uncle Sam: And in your case the inflation's getting out of hand. [He pats **John Bull's** belly.]

John Bull: I admit I have got a slight balance of payments problem.

Uncle Sam: So have I now. Thanks to eating at the same table with you gentlemen.

John Bull: What about our ... [queer innuendo] special relationship? Anglo-Saxon fraternity. That must be worth a few bob.

Uncle Sam: Special relationship? But you've been flirting with that Mamsel Europa. What about European Entry?

John Bull: How d'you do that? In the Kama Sutra, is it?

Uncle Sam: You know what I'm talking about. The Common Market!

John Bull: Oh that. She won't have me. Not till I put my house in order.

Uncle Sam: I'm surprised it's still standing.

John Bull: It's all because of the workers, you know. Wonder if I could send a gun-boat down the mines?

Uncle Sam: What they need is a little taste of unemployment. Let' 'em know who's boss.

John Bull: Blame the workers. I've always found that a good policy. If in doubt, sort 'em out.

[They sing:]

The Solution To All Problems

Inflation spirals to the sky
No-one knows the reason why
And that's why you and I
Must blame the workers
(If in doubt, sort 'em out.)

When our gold reserves go down
And no dollars can be found
We get up off the ground
And blame the workers
(If in doubt, sort 'em out.)

What a very simple song
We are right and they are wrong
Just blame the workers
There's no need to make a fuss
There is nothing wrong with us
Just blame the workers
(If in doubt, sort 'em out.)

John Bull: I know! We'll have this out. In a good old-fashioned British sportsmanlike way. A fight! In the ring.

9. The Big Fight

[**Wally The Worker, George the Foreman,** seconds **Mos Birch, Lady Scanlon-Jones, Mamsel Europa** and **Mr Bi** come into the ring. **Wilson** and **Heath** as judges take u their positions. **John Bull** grabs a mike and announces

John Bull: My lords, ladies and gentlemen, the main bout of the even ing a three-round championship contest between on my rigl in the blue corner, weighing in at 7 stones 3 ounces, th lightweight champion of the management: Crawling Georg the Fearless Foreman! Let's hear your appreciation for th management, ladies and gentlemen. [Pause.] I see. [**Georg** creeps into the ring, knees knocking, he trips, smiles an waves weakly.] And on my left in the red corner, weighin in at 13 stone dead — and so he should be — tonight challenger: Wally the Wonderful Worker! [**Wally** step forward, enormous, confident, no smile but acknowledgin the crowd.] All right, don't overdo it.
Your judges for the evening! On the right from Broadstair and Bexleyheath the Right Honourable Edward 'At stroke' Heath. — Hello, sailor! And on the left — just –

from Huddersfield and Huyton, Mr Harold 'Get back to work' Wilson.

This is a three-round contest, ladies and gentlemen, over three years. The seconds on your right Mr Big and Mamsel Europa. On your left brother Moss Birch and — deputising for her husband, reluctantly called to a trades union conference on Copacabana Beach — Lady Scanlon-Jones!

Now lads, I want a nice clean fight, no leaks to the press, no personal remarks on TV, and above all keep within the law. May the best man win, and if you don't George, you're fired.

Seconds out, Round One! The 1969 Penalty Clauses!

[A bell rings. **The Boxers** come out and circle.]

A word about these two fighters' form. Wally the Worker has put up with no end of hardship in his training over the past 7 years, but with Mr Wilson as current presiding judge and Lady Scanlon-Jones in his corner his chances look better now than for some time.

[**Wally** feints a few blows towards **George.**]

Against that is the new rule-book drawn up by Judge Wilson, 'In Place of Strife.'

[**George** feints towards **Wally.**]

And now I think they're shaping up for the first punch!

[**Wally** lands one on **George,** who reels back towards the ropes.]

Yes there it is! A good strong blow from Wally in the form of a ten percent wage claim. A shilling per hour for every man. Now how will George retaliate?

[As **George** reaches the ropes, **Mr Big** pushes him back in so he butts **Wally** against the ropes. **Mr Big** then proceeds to tie **Wally's** hands to the ropes.]

Oh a nasty one! A seven and a half percent offer from the company but there are strings attached: penalty clauses for bad behaviour!

Wally: 'E's tryin' a tie me 'ands! [He shakes himself free.]

John Bull: Wally was clearly stung by that. He's really got his dander up now. And here it comes!

[**Wally** whacks **George,** who goes down.]

A strike! Against the Penalty Clauses! One! Two weeks!

[**The Seconds** confer.]

'Stick your package,' says Wally, 'a straight wage claim
nothing.' Two and a half weeks! I can see the seconds co
ferring over there — the National Joint Negotiating Con
mittee — probably deciding whether it was a fair blow
not.

[**Wilson** joins them.]

They've brought in Judge Wilson, and the verdict by seve
unions to five is, the blow **was** against the rules. Three week
George's up!

[**George** gets up.]

Moss Birch: Get stuffed, Wilson!
Lady Jones: Our five unions represent 85 per cent of the men!

[**Wally** hits **George** straight down again.]

John Bull: And the strike blow's ratified! Official recognition!

[**George** gets up.]

But George is up again!

[**Wally** and **George** go into a clinch.]

And it's a clinch! Judge Wilson's been called in again. He
clearly being pressed hard by Lady Scanlon-Jones. Th
question is, will she recommend staying on strike to get th
full increase? And it's . . . no!

[**George** bashes **Wally** in the clinch.]

Back to work and renegotiation!
Wally: 'Ere, what's the idea, stewards!

[While his head is turned, **George** bashes **Wally** again.]

John Bull: No increase on the wage offer. [And again.] The disciplinar
procedure the same. [**Wally** whacks **George**.] But against tha
no victimisation of militants. [And again.] The Penalt
Clauses re-phrased to be virtually ineffectual. [And again
And shop stewards on the NJNC! [The bell rings.] An
that's the end of the round. It looks like a clear win o
points for Wally.
Wilson: I agree!
Heath: I don't!
Wally: [To **Lady Jones**] What you do that for?
John Bull: Wally appears to have a complaint to his second, Lad
Jones.
Wally: A bob an hour we said!
Moss Birch: If the bell 'adn't gone, We'd 'ave finished 'im off.

62

Lady Jones: I think it's better intended that way. At least we're ahead on points.

John Bull: Yes indeed, I think Wally can be pretty pleased with that round. [The bell rings.] Round Two: the 1970 Parity Dispute! [**Wally** and **George** come out, circle and feint.] And as they come out this time things still look good for Wally. There's an election coming up and people are predicting a landslide victory for Judge Wilson. Also, Moss Birch's stewards have been building up a huge publicity campaign for this round with parity stickers, leaflets and meetings. [**Wally** whacks **George**.] And there it goes! The claim for parity! Wages equal to those of the car-workers in the Midlands. The question is now: how will George retaliate?

Moss Birch: Watch 'is right, Wally!

[**George** flabbily paws **Wally's** hip.]

John Bull: Was that a punch? It looked more like a caress. And below the belt too! [**Wally** goes down.] One! Two! Three! Four! [**Wally** gets up.] A four pound a week wage offer from the company, and clearly Wally was flabbergasted. Ignored his steward's warning, fell for the tactic and accepted the offer. But now he's up again. [**Wally** and **George** circle. **Wilson** and **Heath** change places.] Oh, I see they've had the election.

Heath: Prices at a stroke!

John Bull: And Judge Heath is now presiding. [The bell rings.] Well, a fascinating round. Clearly won by George with his deceptive blow to the pocket, which some will interpret as a well-timed bribe. The big question, did Wally take a dive in Round Two?

Wilson: He won!

Heath: You shut up. I'm the government now.

Moss Birch: [To **Wally**] You bloody fool!

John Bull: Clearly he's getting a ticking-off from his second. While in the other corner . . .

Europa: You see, Monsieur Big, our secret weapon worked.

Mr Big: Yeh. Payin' de money. Dat really hoit. Take it easy this round, George. [He goes over to see **Heath**.]

John Bull: We know the company's been having trouble with its new Concertina model lately, so they might be quite happy to lie down this round. — I see Mr Big is conferring with Judge Heath.

Mr Big: If we don't get a decision dis round, I'll take my whole show to another arena.

Heath: You can't bribe me. You're always saying that.

Mr Big: You need me on your side, Heath. Don't forget that. [He retires to his corner.]

John Bull: Well, whatever Mr Big's plans, Wally's seconds have bee[n] following a tactics course for their claim prepared by Rusk[in] College, Oxford. [The bell rings.] And out they come[.] Round Three: the 1971 Nine Week Strike! [**Wally** whack[s] **George.**] And straight from the bell Wally goes in with [a] hard claim for parity again. Ten pounds and a thirty-fi[ve] hour week. A very sound punch. [**George** hits **Wally** scor[n]fully.] And George counters straight away with an almo[st] derisory company offer of two pounds. [**Wally** whacks **Georg[e]** who goes down.] And Wally fights back! A strike! We[ll] things have certainly hotted up this round! Unprecedente[d] solidarity from the men! One week! Two weeks!

Mr Big: Unfair punch!

[**The Other Seconds** join him.]

John Bull: And there seems to be an objection from the Management [] corner. The seconds are huddling together in an NJNC mee[t]ing. [**George,** on the floor, weakly waves a fist. **Wally** ignor[es] it.] Meanwhile, in the ring, it looks as though George [is] offering another 1p or so an hour, but Wally's ignoring i[t.] Three weeks! Four weeks! Five! [**Mr Big** and **Scanlo[n]-Jones** go over to **Heath.**] And there's a split between th[e] seconds! Lady Scanlon-Jones has gone over with Mr B[ig] to talk to Judge Heath! Six! Seven! Eight weeks! What [a] strike! Is this a record? [**George** feebly grabs **Wally's** leg[.] And George has feebly grabbed Wally's leg! A four poun[d] offer plus another four over two years, if the unions assur[e] no industrial action. New Year's Day as a paid holiday[.] Nine weeks!

[**Lady Scanlon-Jones** crosses the ring to shake **Wally's** han[d] and then Mr Big's.]

Lady Jones: It's over! — Well done, you muscular fellow!

Moss Birch: Where you goin'? You silly cow!

John Bull: What's this? Lady Jones has jumped the gun! Gone ove[r] Moss Birch's head before the count's finished!

Lady Jones: Bad luck, Mr Big. Don't forget equal pay for women.

Mr Big: It's a deal. And you're disqualified. — Dis broad shouldn[t] be in de ring!

John Bull: How true. And how convenient. — Ladies and gentleme[n,] after a disqualification, retaining his title as champion o[f] the management, George the Foreman!

Wilson: [Leaning forward.] Not **the** George Foreman?

John Bull: Do you mind? — Mr Heath, would you step up to presen[t] the trophy please? [He takes a chamber-pot.]

Heath: Oh heow nice. What is it?

John Bull:	The Industrial Relations Act Piss-pot.
Heath:	Oh! [To **Mr Big** and **George**] You can put it under your bed. Give the reds something to think about. Haw-haw-haw!
John Bull:	For the loser, this key to Europe, guaranteed to fit Mamsel Europa's chastity belt. [He gives it to **Mamsel Europa**.]
Wally:	Is that for me?
Europa:	Yes, and you will find me a very expensive lady to keep.
Moss Birch:	It's a fiddle! Fix! Fix!
John Bull:	Your appreciation, ladies and gentlemen, for the contestants!
Heath:	Here here! And from now on it's plain sailing all the way. All hands pulling together, charting a new course into Europe. And with me at the helm, you can be sure of shipwreck!

10. Rising Prices in the Supermarket

[Two middle-aged housewives, **Annie** and **Lil,** in the supermarket, with their baskets.]

Lil:	'Ere Annie, look at them eggs. They gawn up double since 1970.
Annie:	I know, Lil. An' to fink old 'Eaffy said 'e'd cut prices at a stroke. 'Im an' 'is bleedin' Common Market.
Lil:	D'you know, I went round Tesco's the other day, saw a loaf marked 13p, I thought thass a bit steep, so I went round Finefare. 14p there. All right, I fought, back to Tesco's. By the time I got there they'd put theirs up to bleedin' 15p!
Annie:	'S yer three-bob loaf en it, lovey.
Lil:	My ol' man goes frough the roof when I ask 'im for me 'ousekeepin'.
Annie:	You're lucky. We ain' 'ad a roof since them winds last Friday night.
Lil:	Bleedin' council-'ouses.
Annie:	I know, love. We fought we'd save up for an 'ouse — of our own. We reckoned if we saved a third of our wages we could pay awff the mortgage. But mortgages 've gawn up double since then! We'd 'ave to save 'arf our wages now! Well I mean, the buildin' society's not standin' fer that, are they.
Lil:	Why don't yer buy yer own council-'ouse? Ol' Teeffy's allowin' that, en 'e?
Annie:	Yeh. Trouble is, 'e's not buildin' any more, is 'e. I fink about all them young couples wiv kids. They can't get a place anywhere else, the Council list's as long as yer arm, so all we'd be doin' is deprivin' the young 'uns. It was 'ard

Lil: Fings don't get better, do they.

Annie: Spite a what they say.

Lil: 'Ere, 'ave you noticed the number of men out shoppin' lately? Used t' be all women 'ere. Now there's just as many men.

Annie: All laid awff, en't they.

Lil: Gawblimey, it's gettin' like the thirties. 'Ere, Big's ain't layin' men awff, are they? No car-workers in 'ere, are there?

Annie: Not yet, love, no.

Lil: Mind you, bound to come. The roads is so full they won't get any more cars on 'em soon, rate they're goin'.

Annie: Either that or we'll all choke t' death on the fumes.

Lil: Long as they don't lay the men awff, thass what I say.

Annie: They should go over t' makin' buses. We could do wiv more a them. You can wait free-quarters of an hour fer one these days.

Lil: An' then pay frough the nose fer the privilege.

Annie: Shockin'.

Lil: I know, love.

Annie: Well I'm blowed. Look at that. While we been standin' 'ere talkin', them eggs've gawn up 2p!

11. The Bad Dream and Cold Reality of Trade War

[**Mr Big,** alone, but with **The Guy Asleep Under The Blanket** in his original position, switches on his TV.]

Mr Big: Ah-h, dis is de life. Prices findin' a nice high level. People pullin' in deir belts at home so we can pour money into factories overseas. In nice democratic countries like Spain and South Africa. And an Industrial Relations Act to stop de woikers challengin' dis lovely status quo. [He starts.] Who's dat? [He sees **The Guy Asleep Under the Blanket**.] — Oh, you're still here. People are makin' fortunes while you're dozin' your life away, brother! — Still, it's not a bad idea. [He yawns.] Ah-h, what a wonderful woild. [He falls asleep, snores lightly.]

[**Toyota, Volkswagen, Renault** and **Fiat** sneak in on tip-toe.]

VW: Sshh!

Toyota: Here we are at last! Mr Big's famous opelations centre! All his seclets — ours for the taking.

[They start taking his maps and charts down, rifling his drawers, stealing everything.]

VW: Vunce ve know vere hiss new markets are, zey become our new markets too!

66

Toyota: Mr Big teach most important lesson of all: look after Number One!

Renault: Zet's right. Eets every man for 'imself from now on — [To **Fiat**] Leave zat alone, I saw eet first!

Fiat: What-a you talk about? Free enterprise isa free enterprise.

VW: Zet's right! End Fee-Doubleyou's sales in ze USA are efen beatink Mr Big's himself!

Renault: Eet's all right for you. Some of us don't 'ave such strong currencies.

Fiat: Whata you talk about? We all gota problem. Labour problems, inflationa problems, we alla need growinga profits, we alla needa bigger markets. That'sa why we're here!

[They search his files.]

Toyota: How Mr Big deal with labour ploblems. Velly important question. No more cheap labour for Japanese. Little workers get too big for boots.

VW: How does he kip hiss vages down?

Fiat: Howa do you bribe a government?

Renault: Which countrees is 'e goieeng to next? — Ah! I've found eet! [He holds up a piece of paper.]

Fiat: Let me see!

VW: End me!

Toyota: Me also please!

[They crowd round **Renault.**]

VW: Sous Efrika?

Fiat: Spaina?

Toyota: Lhodesia?

Renault: Factories in, er, Buenos Aires, Karachi, Bangkok, Djakarta, Manila, Istanbul, Taiwan...

Toyota: Yahay!

[The phone flashes.]

Renault: Look, ze phone ees ringeeng!

VW: [Picking it up swiftly.] Hello? Ja? No. No. No. No. Hef you tieed Volkswagen. Much more efficient. OK. Auf wiedersehen. — Ha!

Renault: You crook!

Fiat: Letters! [He rips open one of **Mr Big's** letters, reads and slips it in his pocket. The others follow suit. **Mr Big** stirs in his sleep.]

Mr Big: [In his sleep] Agh! They're robbin' me! Pappy! Pappy! They're robbin' me! Help!

Pappy: Heh-heh-heh! I told you this would happen, son. But yo wouldn't listen, you stubborn boy.

Mr Big: You gotta do something! Help!

Pappy: Nothing I can do, son. Things is gettin' worse fast. Yahoo

Mr Big: You sound like you're enjoying this, Pa. Not the End the Line, Pa, not the Bad Harvest!

Pappy: Just around the corner, son. The storm's gettin' worse, th markets are floodin', an' everyone's tryin' to steal each other barns. Crazy! I love it!

Mr Big: What can I do, Pappy? You gotta help me!

Pappy: Sorry, son. I got some oats of my own t' sow.

Mr Big: Ain't it time for your nap?

Pappy: No time for sleepin' now things is hottin' up, boy. I'r beginnin' to enjoy life again. Yahoo! So long, son!

Mr Big: [Still asleep.] Pa! Pa! Pappy! — He's gone! Oh! Help Help, police! Help!

[As **The Others** begin to emerge again, **Uncle Sam** come in, with a few policeman's attributes. **The Others** duck down

Mr Big: Uncle Sam! Good to see you! You're the world's policeman you gotta help me!

Uncle Sam: Goddamit, ain't folks got no respect for private property n more? Everyone invading everyone else's markets, the world going mad!

Mr Big: I'm being burgled!

Uncle Sam: Who isn't? I better get back and protect my own property

Mr Big: Don't go! I need you! You gotta help me!

Uncle Sam: Where were you in the thirties, Big, when I needed you? It's all selfishness. Folk making a mockery of internationa currency agreements — up and down, devalue, revalue, floa this, float that. And all against the dollar. You're drainin my reserves!

Mr Big: I got problems, Uncle Sam, bad problems. Worse'n I ever had before. I've always been ahead of things. Now I feel ou of date.

Uncle Sam: Your car's being overtaken, Big. All the new manufacturers got the new technology an' it just ain't worth my while modernising you. I got my own balance of payments problem, remember.

Mr Big: Desperate measures, that's what we need! Desperate measures.

Uncle Sam: Too darn right. I'm taking this back. [He picks up the barometer.]

Mr Big: Not the barometer! Not now! Anything but that!

Uncle Sam: I'm floatin' the dollar, Big. It can't stand the strain no more.

Mr Big: No!

Uncle Sam: This barometer was gentlemen's agreement, and you guys ain't gentlemen no more. It's trade war, Big. An' I'm throwin' in my world policeman's badge. Going home to polish my guns. I got my own family to protect. [He goes.]

Mr Big: No-o!

[**The Others** come out of hiding.]

Toyota: Aiee! Incle Sam take away barometer! Now evelyone in shtook.

VW: Donner und Blitzen! Ve're goink to hef to get tough, boys.

Renault: Merde!

Fiat: Praps we shoulda give in to zea workers. Go socialist.

VW: Everyone knows you Eyeties are cowards.

Mr Big: [Waking.] Oh my God, what a terrible dream! [**The Others** hide again.] Thank God it was only a dream. — The barometer! Where is it? Don't say it's really happening! My charts! My maps! My files! Where are they?

[**The Others** spring out of hiding.]

Toyota: Yahay!

Mr Big: What are you doing here?

VW: Ve're movink faster, Mr Big. Ze days off your dominance are ofer!

Mr Big: So it is war!

Renault: Unfortunately, yes.

Mr Big: Each of us against the other.

Renault: And all of us against:

Mr Big: The consumer?

Renault: And:

Mr Big: The woiker!

Renault: Zat's right.

Mr Big: Goddamit, I gotta start makin' some bombs. Milk bottles. A few molotov cocktails is what's needed here.

Renault: OK!

[They all hunt round, find milk bottles and bits of rag.]

Fiat: I gota one!

VW: Ent me!

Toyota: Me also!

Renault: Voila! — And may ze best man win!

[They stand ready to throw them at each other.]

Mr Big: Goddamit, we've forgotten the petrol. Where is it? Where's the petrol?

Abdul: Thought old Abdul was asleep, did you? You want petr
I've been sitting on it all this time. Waiting. Old Ar
proverb: never disturb man asleep. Might be sitting
hornets' nest.

Mr Big: This is no time for proverbs, Abdul, we need that stuf

Abdul: You need it, you pay for it. What am I bid?

Mr Big: More'n the others!

Renault: More zan 'eem!

VW: More zan zat!

Toyota: More still!

Fiat: More-a! More-a!

Abdul: You need it, you pay for it.

12. The Working Class, January 1974.

[**An Actor** comes on, dressed as a miner.]

Miner: That's what the miner said. You need it, you pay for it.
that point at least he agreed with old Abdul. The Arab h
oil, he gave coal. He'd worn his fingers to the bone, he
coughed his lungs up, given his life. And when he stopp
the country stopped. Remember that.

Then as now he'd never had a fair deal out of this count
so the Tory government's policy of wage restraint amount
to legalised injustice. An Industrial Relations Act, la
against picketing and state control of wages. But twice
three years the miner burst that injustice wide open
with solidarity and determination, the workers' best weapo
Owners, management and government were like corner
rats — dangerous. Their crisis and no course open to the
but a battle, to preserve their privilege and their profits. Th
blame the worker, try to make him pay for their mistak
by beating down his wage claims, attacking the trad
unions, decimating social services and making him redunda
Decent food, housing and social services — in a civilised a
democratic land a worker would have a right to the
things. But only by standing up solid and determined will
ever get them.

[**Actors** as Carworker and his Wife come on.]

Wife: But where does the worker's wife stand when her husband
on strike or short time? She's still got to buy the food, pa
the rent. What if Mr Big threatens to close his factory dov

for ever? What if he threatens to move out?

Carworker: As long as he's squeezing nine cars a year out of us, he'll stay, don't worry. The threat to move is just a tactic. Not that he hasn't got the power to if he wants, especially with an oil crisis. But that's all the more reason to keep an eye on him. It's men's jobs he's dealing in, men's lives, not motor cars. And it's up to us to make sure he recognises that fact. If the industry's winding down, we do ourselves no good by helping him. The miner's right. If they want coal out of him, let them pay him. If they want cars out of us, let them pay us.

All: [They sing:]

> Yesterday's story, all in the past
> Yesterday's story, class against class
> Why should we tell it? What's it all for?
> Do yesterday's battles matter no more?
>
> The same situation is happening today
> The same confrontation over hours and pay
> The struggle continues just like in the past
> That's today's story, how long will it last?
>
> And what of tomorrow? What do we need?
> Control of the factories, control of our lives
> To hell with the bosses and the rest of their breed
> We'll continue the struggle, that's the war that we wage
> We'll continue the struggle till the system is changed.

71

Steve Gooch

Female Transport

Six working class women have been convicted of petty crimes in early nineteenth century London. **Female Transport** is a tough and realistic account of their six month voyage to Australia, locked together in a ship's cell.

From their tentative and desperate first steps in coming to terms with each other and the oppression of their all-male jailers, to their final disembarkation as a tight-knit bunch of hardened rebels at Sydney, the play shows what effects decisions made above deck produce on the 'cargo' below.

'Charts the growing spirit of resistance and self-awareness among six particular women as they come to recognize clearly where their strength lies.'
Naseem Khan, *Time Out*

Steve Gooch is actively involved in community theatre. He has written two other plays published by Pluto Press, **Female Transport** and **Will Wat, If Not, What Will?**

Steve Gooch

Will Wat, If Not, What Will?

A workshop play about Wat Tyler and the peasant uprising of 1381. It tells the peasants' side of the story—the side not normally told in the history books.

It finds the peasants up against Edward III's militarism, the increasing ambition of the rising merchant class, the Black Death and the notorious Statute of Labourers—the first legal restriction in England on the free bargaining power of labour. The uprising itself is followed, from its spontaneous and almost accidental beginnings. A leadership gradually emerges including Wat Tyler and the lay preacher John Ball.

"**Will Wat** doesn't show you the Peasants' Revolt of 1381, it involves you in it . . . By the end of the evening I felt proud to have shared history with the peasants of Erith, Brentford and Romney Marsh; and ready to raise a bill-hook against all oppressors . . ."
John Mortimer, *The Observer*